SLOW COOKER
RECIPE BOOK UK

200 Delicious & Quick recipes to satisfy all your cravings while keeping your health in balance, including Side dishes, Desserts and More

By **Priscilla Cannon**

© Copyright 2021 by PRISCILLA CANNON - All rights reserved.

This document is geared towards providing exact and reliable information in regards to the topic and issue covered. The publication is sold with the idea that the publisher is not required to render accounting, officially permitted, or otherwise, qualified services. If advice is necessary, legal or professional, a practiced individual in the profession should be ordered.

- From a Declaration of Principles which was accepted and approved equally by a Committee of the American Bar Association and a Committee of Publishers and Associations.

In no way is it legal to reproduce, duplicate, or transmit any part of this document in either electronic means or in printed format. Recording of this publication is strictly prohibited and any storage of this document is not allowed unless with written permission from the publisher. All rights reserved.

The information provided herein is stated to be truthful and consistent, in that any liability, in terms of inattention or otherwise, by any usage or abuse of any policies, processes, or directions contained within is the solitary and utter responsibility of the recipient reader. Under no circumstances will any legal responsibility or blame be held against the publisher for any reparation, damages, or monetary loss due to the information herein, either directly or indirectly.

Respective authors own all copyrights not held by the publisher.

The information herein is offered for informational purposes solely, and is universal as so. The presentation of the information is without contract or any type of guarantee assurance.

The trademarks that are used are without any consent, and the publication of the trademark is without permission or backing by the trademark owner. All trademarks and brands within this book are for clarifying purposes only and are the owned by the owners themselves, not affiliated with this document.

Table Of Contents

INTRODUCTION 8

CHAPTER 1: A GUIDE ABOUT SLOW COOKER 10
- 1.1 How Does a Slow Cooker Work? 11
- 1.2 History of Slow Cooker 12
- 1.3 Parts of Slow Cooker 12
- 1.4 What to Cook in a Slow Cooker? 13
- 1.5 Benefits of Using a Slow Cooker 15
- 1.6 How to Make the Most of Your Slow Cooker? 16
- 1.7 Tips to Make Food in Slow Cooker 17
- 1.8 Instructions for Preparing Foods for Slow Cooker .. 17
- 1.9 Slow Cooker Safety 18

CHAPTER 2: APPETIZERS AND SOUPS 20
1. Cordon Bleu Soup 21
2. Cheesy Potato Soup 22
3. Pumpkin Sausage Soup 23
4. Bean Soup with Spinach 24
5. Butternut Squash Soup 25
6. Pork Bean Soup 26
7. Pumpkin Soup 27
8. Potato And Cheddar Creamy Soup 28
9. Pumpkin And Black Bean Soup 29
10. Lentil Soup 30
11. Lime Chicken Soup With Rice 31
12. Shrimp Chowder 32
13. Vegetable Soup With Wild Rice 33
14. Chicken Tomato Chili Soup 34
15. Cabbage Soup 35
16. Chicken Meatballs With Mozzarella Stuffing 36
17. Cheese Queso 37
18. Mini BBQ Smoky 38
19. Honey Glazed Chipotle Meatballs 39
20. Bacon Dip Chicken Ranch 40
21. Cheese Sauce Salsa 41
22. Mixed Nut Ranch 42
23. Mixed Nutty Snack 43
24. Lettuce And Beefy Wrap 44
25. Sour And Sweet Chicken Wings 45

CHAPTER 3: MEAT MEALS 46
1. Pulled BBQ Chicken 47
2. Simple Chicken Casserole 48
3. Delicious Baked Chicken 49
4. Creamy Chicken with Mushroom Sauce 50
5. Garlic Honey Chicken 51
6. Lamb Shanks With Burgundy Sauce 52
7. Tender Lamb With Tomato Stew 53
8. Mint lamb with Mashed Potatoes 54
9. Lamb Shoulder With Mint Gravy 55
10. Lamb Shanks With Rosemary 56
11. Pork Fillet 57
12. Ham With Maple Syrup 58
13. Pork And Apple Casserole 59
14. Pork Chops With Veggies 60
15. Roasted Pork 61
16. Beef Lasagna 62
17. Beef Chili 63
18. Beef Dumplings And Stew 64
19. Beef Casserole with Red wine 65
20. Beef Braised Ribs 66
21. Tender Turkey With Herbs 67
22. Turkey Casserole 68
23. Hot Turkey Chili 69
24. Milky Turkey Stew 70
25. Turkey Delight 71

CHAPTER 4: FISH MEALS 72
1. Creamy Fish Chowder 73
2. Chickpeas With Fish Stew 74
3. Easy Clam Chowder 75
4. Easy Smoked Coley 76
5. Delicious Thai Fish Curry 77
6. Jamaican Fish Stew 78
7. Salmon With Rice 79
8. Easy Fish Stew 80
9. Fish With Tomato Sauce 81
10. Italian Herb Salmon 82
11. Salmon With Dill And lemon 83
12. Salmon Stew And Coconut Curry 84
13. Mixed Fish Pie 85
14. White Fish Gratin 86
15. Salmon Chowder 87
16. Fish Chowder With Shrimps 88
17. Salmon With Chili And Lime 89
18. Delicious Seafood Stew 90
19. Fish Risotto 91
20. Fish Stew In Coconut Milk 92
21. Marinara Cod 93
22. Salmon With Lentil Curry 94
23. Fish Stew With Garlic and Pancetta 95
24. Cod With Red Curry 96

25. Monkfish Curry 97
26. Kerala Fish Coconut Curry 98
27. Cooked Shrimps With Rice 99

CHAPTER 5: VEGETARIAN MEALS 100

1. Quinoa With Corn Chowder 101
2. Pea Risotto And Green Beans 102
3. Slow Cooker Chili Veggie 103
4. Cauliflower And Pumpkin Curry 104
5. Vegan Chili With Beans 105
6. Cheesy Chickpeas 106
7. Potato And Leek Soup 107
8. Quorn Chili Veggie Bowl 108
9. Chili And Bean Combo 109
10. Easy Vegetable Soup 110
11. Salty Baked Potatoes 111
12. Aubergine, Mushroom And Potato Curry 112
13. Red Lentil And Pumpkin Soup 113
14. Beans And Barley Curry 114
15. Chia And Blueberry Quinoa Bowl 115
16. Creamy Leek Soup 116
17. Easy Forest Risotto 117
18. Cheesy Sweet Corns 118
19. Tomato Soup 119
20. Creamy Potatoes 120
21. Carrot Glaze 121
22. Slow Cooker Cassoulet 122
23. Delicious Spaghetti Squash 123
24. Slow Cooker Vegan Soup 124
25. Cheese Risotto Primavera 125

CHAPTER 6: GLUTEN-FREE RECIPES 126

1. Chicken Gravy 127
2. Tomato Soup 128
3. Onion Gravy With Sausage 129
4. Creamy Potato Sausage 130
5. Roasted Lamb 131
6. Sweet Potatoes Soup 132
7. Cheesy Chicken Broccoli Rice 133
8. Bangers and Mash 134
9. Shepherd's Pie 135
10. Beef Stew 136
11. Cuban Beef 137
12. Bolognese 138
13. Apple, Sausage and Bean Casserole 139
14. Apple Butter 140
15. Chili Con Carne 141
16. Chicken Casserole 142
17. Sweet Potato Turkey Stew 143
18. Gluten-Free Sausages and Potatoes Stew 144
19. Sweet Potato, Spinach and Peas Curry 145
20. Lentil and Sausages Stew 146
21. Turkish Hash 147
22. Meatballs 148
23. BBQ Pork 149
24. Chicken Tacos Queso 150
25. Chicken Carbonara 151

CHAPTER 7: SIDE DISHES 152

1. Mashed Potatoes 153
2. Baked Potatoes 154
3. Wild Rice Mushrooms 155
4. Carrots Glazed 156
5. Baked Haricot Beans 157
6. Baked Cannellini Bean 158
7. Sweetcorn 159
8. Cauliflower and Potato Mash 160
9. Spaghetti Squash 161
10. Cheesy Potatoes 162
11. Courgette 163
12. Refried Pinto Beans 164
13. Pomegranate and Vanilla Brussels Sprout 165
14. Vegetable Mashup 166
15. Clapshot 167
16. Peppered Bacon With Ranch Beans 168
17. Stovies 169
18. Orange Sage Sweet Potato With Bacon 170
19. Creamy Spinach 171
20. Cornbread And Sausage 172
21. Macaroni and Cheese 173
22. Creamy Chicken Peas With Mushrooms 174
23. Sweet and Tart Red Cabbage 175
24. Thanksgiving Stuffing 176
25. Cranberry Sauce 177

CHAPTER 8: SNACK RECIPES 178

1. Easy Chex Mix 179
2. Crispy Chicken Taquitos 180
3. Chicken Pita Bites 181
4. Beef Ranch And Cheesy Potatoes 182
5. Honey Pork 183
6. Barbeque Kielbasa 184
7. Chicken Buffalo Meatballs 185
8. Chicken Wings 186
9. Barbeque Small Smokies 187
10. Mozzarella Meatballs 188
11. Creamy Cheese Chicken Taquitos 189
12. Spicy Meatballs 190

13. Pork Tacos 191
14. Garlic Shrimps 192
15. Ham Balls 193
16. Mashed Potatoes 194
17. Nuts Cereal Mix 195
18. Boiled Nuts 196
19. Spicy Drumsticks 197
20. Chicken Lettuce Cups 198
21. Warm Baked Potatoes 199
22. Tender and Delicious Sausages 200
23. Spicy Chicken Wings With Cheese Dip 201
24. Beef And Parmesan Dumplings 202
25. Delicious Stuffed Peppers 203

CHAPTER 9: DESSERT RECIPES 204
1. Rice Pudding 205
2. Black Forest Cake 206
3. Apple Pudding 207
4. Chocolate Cake 208
5. Apple Crisp 209
6. Orange Sponge Chocolate Pudding 210
7. Banana Foster 211
8. Warm Cross Bun Loaf Pudding 212
9. Peanut Butter Cake 213
10. Berries Compote 214
11. Cinnamon Rolls 215
12. Blackberry Cobbler 216
13. Peanut Butter Blondies 217
14. Nut Clusters 218
15. Mixed Berry Cake 219
16. Fudge Bars 220
17. Spice Apple Sauce Cake 221
18. Peachy Cobbler 222
19. Coffee Cake 223
20. Caramel Cream Dessert 224
21. Apple Puree 225
22. Peanut Butter and Chocolate Pudding 226
23. Coconut Cake 227
24. Cream Brulee 228
25. Peach Cake 229

CONCLUSION 230

Introduction

It's another very cold day outside, and after a long, exhausting day at the office, the last thing you want to do is work over the stove, slaving away to prepare a good dinner. Thanks to your preparations, you may enter into your house to the smell of stew drifting through the air, luring you in for a hearty meal that is waiting for you. Even though no one has come home, your dinner is almost done due to your slow cooker. A slow cooker is a tiny electrical device that has been a fixture of many households for more than 30 years. Its principles are founded on the concept of slow cooking. It's easy to understand its idea, place food in its container or enclosed space and let it cook slowly. The technique is employed in barbeque pits and pig roasts, where moderate temperatures and a long cooking period make the meat soft and fall off the bone. This may be accomplished with dry heat, such as in an oven or roaster, or it can be accomplished with wet heat, such as by including liquid into the cooking process. As a result of the fact that they stay sealed during the cooking process, slow cookers make innovative use of moisture. As the meal cooks and releases steam, condensation accumulates within the device, which serves as a baster for the dish. It allows you to prepare meals while away from home, thus saving you both time and energy. Isn't it nice to come home to a cooked dinner waiting for you and your family when you get home from work each day? In addition to being efficient for you, the slow cooker is also efficient for your house. An average-sized slow cooker consumes about the same electricity as light bulbs. Since it cooks with controlled heat, it consumes less energy. Furthermore, since it is an appliance designed to be used unattended, there is no need to be concerned about it while you are away. This book has a guide about slow cookers and 200 delicious recipes for you.

CHAPTER 1:

A Guide About Slow Cooker

Slow cookers are electrical gadgets that plug into a wall outlet and cook liquid-based meals over a lengthy period, typically four hours or more, by using moderate heat over a long period. The benefit of doing so is that you may prepare dinner in the morning and leave it untouched during the day, returning to a ready-cooked supper in the evening. The devices are available for purchase for as little as a tenner or as many as a few hundred pounds, depending on the model you choose. Different models satisfy a variety of requirements and have a variety of optional features.

Slow cooker recipes are very popular, and they can be used to prepare a variety of delectable curries, quiches, soup, and stews, among other dishes. Slow cookers prepare nutritious weekday dinners and larger cuts of beef or lamb that need the most cooking time necessary to get the finest results. This is a somewhat old-fashioned concept, but it's fair to say that the outcomes are ideal for a family with a lot on their plate. Although you will still need to put the ingredients together, using a slow cooker can significantly decrease the amount of time you spend in the kitchen when you get home from work. Create a wonderful dinner the night before or the morning of, and you'll be able to come home to a lovely supper ready and waiting for you.

Using a slow cooker has been around for generations, and the electrical cooker initially gained popularity in the 1970s kitchen, when the first cookers of this type were available in fashionable hues like avocado and goldenrod. However, when microwaves became popular a few years later, the slow cooker was left in the dust as consumers began zapping their meals in the microwave.

Although the trend has shifted back to slow cooking, a slew of new cookbooks provide a range of delectable recipes for this appliance. Manufacturers created newer, more attractive versions of the gadget, which resulted in its revival as a must-have appliance for time-pressed chefs during the past decade. In the next part, we'll look at how a slow cooker works.

1.1 How Does a Slow Cooker Work?

Base with the heating element, vessel, and a glass cover are the components of this device. The vessel is the container in which the food is put for cooking. It is often made of thick stoneware, ensuring that the heat is steady, level, and stable.

Cooking Method

Slow cooking is comparable to cooking on a stovetop or in a dutch oven. The heat starts at the bottom of a slow cooker and rises the sides before distributing the food. The steam produced by the heat forms a vacuum seal between the lid and the pan. Low and constant cooking temperatures aid in the retention of moisture throughout the cooking process. The liquid does not evaporate or get more concentrated as a result of this.

Machine Settings

Most machines have three settings; low, high, and warm. It is possible to cook at temperatures ranging from 170°F to 210°F. Both the low and high settings will reach a maximum temperature of 215°F. However, the low option will cycle on and off at that degree more often. As a result, the food will be cooked shorter on the high setting than on the lower one.

In the warm setting, the temperature will range between 165 and 175°F.

- **For Roasts:** Use the low or high setting on your oven.
- **Warm Mode:** This is ideal for keeping dishes warm at parties.
- **For Stews and Soups:** Use the low or high heat settings.
- **For Lean Proteins:** Chicken thighs, breasts, or pork loin are excellent choices for braising on low heat, with the chicken breasts being bone-in.
- **For Fish and Meat:** Poaching is the best method for cooking shellfish, fish, and protein-rich meats such as chicken breast since it cooks more quickly than other proteins.
- **For Beef:** Braising is a great method for cooking harder, less costly pieces of meat that include marbling, such as shoulder cuts of beef or pig. Collagen in the meat's connective tissues is broken down, tenderized, and transformed into gelatin during the low-and-slow cooking method, resulting in an exceptionally delicious by-product.

1.2 History of Slow Cooker

The slow cooker evolved from an electrical bean pot, first used to soak dry beans in the 1960s and then cook rice. The Electrical bean pot, manufactured by small-appliance company West Bend, is a knockoff product developed by competitor Nixon Corporation. After acquiring Nixon, the rival firm, controlled by Jarden, modified the Beanery and marketed it as the slow cooker, a slow cooker that could cook whole meals in a single pot. The cooker quickly gained popularity as a time- and money-saving gadget for working women who wished to cook simultaneously, and the brand became as ubiquitous as Kleenex. In fact, according to a 2002 Betty Crocker Kitchen survey, more than 80% of homes in the US possessed at least one slow cooker.

1.3 Parts of Slow Cooker

The following are the three essential components of a slow cooker:

- An outer shell is used to protect anything within.
- An inner container is a container inside a container.
- It has a lid.

The outside casing is made of metal, and it includes low-wattage heating coils, which are the component responsible for cooking the food. These heating coils are fully enclosed by the outer casing, ensuring that the food is not burned. The inner container, which is often referred to as a crock, is constructed of glazed ceramic and is designed to fit within the heating element made of metal. You may be able to separate the cooking crock from the exterior shell in certain versions. The third component of the device is a crock with a domed cover that fits snugly on top of it.

Working Methodology

The appliance cooks by a combination of wattage and cooking time settings. Upon activation, the electrical coils heat up and begin to conduct indirect heat transfer from the exterior casing to the gap between the base wall and the stoneware container. This indirect heat raises the temperature of the crock to anywhere between 180 and 300°F. Cooking the Ingredients in the crock at a low temperature for many hours until the meat is fully cooked using this technique of heat transmission. Steam is released when the food cooks and the lid prevent it from escaping. As a result of the condensation, a vacuum seal is created between the lid and the rim of the crock, which helps retain moisture while also speeding up cooking time. The lid is essential to the cooking process. These cookers are usually equipped with three settings: low, high, and off. When using a programmed slow cooker, the device will automatically switch to the warm setting once the food has been cooked to ensure that the meal remains at the correct temperature.

1.4 What to Cook in a Slow Cooker?

Slow cookers are a convenient method to prepare meat and veggies at the same time.

Meat

Meats are one of the most popular things to cook in this cooker, but they must be thawed beforehand or take excessive time to cook in it. To eliminate any germs in meat, it must be cooked to a temperature of 140 °F as soon as possible after being cut up. Before serving, always check that the internal temperature of the meat is within the acceptable range of temperatures. When cooking chicken, make sure the skin is still connected to the bird since this will keep the flesh juicy throughout the process.

Vegetables

Preparing veggies for slow cooking may take longer than preparing the meat since it is essential to cut them consistently to cook evenly throughout the meal. In addition, since vegetables cook at a slower rate than meat, stack the veggies on the bottom of the pot when making stews or veggie meals, such as chili.

Soups and Stews

These are some of the finest slow cooker meals since the slow cooker is intended to simmer on a low setting for extended periods, making them ideal for the slow cooker. Add enough water to cover the soup components completely, and if you need to add additional liquid while cooking, bring it to a boil first so that it doesn't decrease the boiling temperature of the soup.

Sauces and Dips

These cookers excel in the preparation of dips and spreads, among other things. Low heat keeps a cheese-based dip warm without burning the components, and keeping a dip warm at a low heat avoids the ingredients from congealing when serving at a gathering.

Grains

Slow cooker grains may be a surprising way to make use of your slow cooker. Porridge made from oats, wheat, or rice may be prepared ahead of time and served hot and nutritiously in the morning.

Bread

It is possible to bake bread and bread-based meals such as stuffing in this cooker, and the low heat setting aids in the rising of the bread dough.

Desserts

These are perhaps another unexpected area for slow-cooking. While rice and tapioca puddings may seem like a no-brainer, slow cookers may also be used to create hot fruit desserts, such as fruit cobblers and fruit cakes.

Important Tips

The nature of certain components and their tolerance for the slow-cooking procedure necessitates the addition of Ingredients after the cooking period in some recipes. Spices and herbs may get overly concentrated throughout the cooking process, so be sure to correct their concentrations once it's finished.

Similarly, certain vegetables, dairy items, and seafood may lose their taste and texture if they are cooked for an excessive amount of time; thus, if the recipe asks for adding them towards the end of the cooking process, be sure to follow the instructions completely and thoroughly.

1.5 Benefits of Using a Slow Cooker

Using a slow cooker to make a healthy dinner is a wonderful way to save time and still eat well. Combine all of the ingredients in the morning, place them in the slow cooker, and supper is ready by the end of the day without creating a lot of mess or washing many dishes.

- This device needs just a little amount of power to perform its functions as compared to a normal oven, a slow cooker consumes much less energy, and as a result, it will not heat a whole kitchen in the manner of an oven.
- When it comes to cooking, using a slow cooker may also be a cost-effective option since it allows you to utilize lower-cost types of meat.
- Since condensation works as a self-baster in the slow cooker, usually harder pieces of meat become soft.
- Just because you are saving time and money does not imply that you are compromising food quality.
- Using a slow cooker, vegetables can absorb stock and spices, resulting in a more flavorful dish.
- When compared to blasting your oven or cooktop for hours on end, this low-wattage device consumes a fraction of the energy of other appliances.
- Cooking in modest quantities is also a safe method that does not heat your whole home, but it does make your house smell wonderful.
- Meats that are tougher to cook benefit from low and slow cooking as well, allowing you to save money by not having to spend a lot of time and money on restaurant-quality meals that would otherwise take all day to prepare.
- Everyone is very busy and don't have the luxury of spending the whole day in the kitchen, no matter how much some of us would want to.
- Slow cooking is a safe method of preparing meals that can be set and forgotten, allowing us to free up hours to do other essential tasks or spend time with family.
- It's also extremely easy to prepare the ingredients before putting them in the slow cooker for cooking.
- Using the slow cooker to prepare low-fat dishes, you may poach or braise them, simmer them in broths or water, or season them with spices and other flavorings.

- The high and low-temperature settings on the device enable you to customize the cooking temperature for the amount of time you want the dish to be prepared. Even though cooking on low is perfectly safe, the Us Department of Agriculture advises cooking on high for an hour to verify that the food is fully cooked before lowering the heat.

1.6 How to Make the Most of Your Slow Cooker?

A decent rule of thumb is that the slow cooker usually has to be filled at least halfway before it will work well, but it should not be filled more than 2/3 of the way before operating successfully.

Cooking Options

Typically, there are just two cooking options: high and low. Some units also feature a keep-warm option for when you're hosting a party or hosting guests. The setting you select is determined by the oven model you have, how quickly you want to cook the meal, and the kind of Ingredients you're cooking with.

Time Range

The majority of slow cooker recipes include a time range. The amount of time required will vary depending on several factors such as the temperature, thickness, kind of meat, and how full the cooker is. Generally speaking, the low-temperature setting takes twice as long as the high-temperature setting. Prepare a little more time before serving if you need to cook for a little longer than anticipated.

Slow Cooker Cooking Equipment

For the slow cooker, there is a variety of equipment and accessories to choose from as well.

- Fat Separator
- Cooking liners
- Meat thermometer
- Tongs made of metal
- Meat shredder claws

1.7 Tips to Make Food in Slow Cooker

While making food in a slow cooker, you need to take care of some points. Some of them are described below.

- Do not remove the lid from the container. Try not to be tempted to open the lid over and over again. A properly fastened cap produces steam, which helps to form a seal. Each time you raise the lid and let the steam escape, you may add up to 25 minutes to your cooking time, so don't check unless specifically told to do so by the recipe.
- When cooking with an infrared thermometer, check whether food is done at the beginning of the suggested cooking time for the temperature setting and allow it to cook longer if necessary.
- Remove the components of the slow cooker within an hour after fully cooking it, and then refrigerate any leftovers to ensure that the food is safe to eat.
- Food should not be reheated in the slow cooker. It is preferable to heat the ingredients on the stovetop or in the microwave before adding them back to the slow cooker.

1.8 Instructions for Preparing Foods for Slow Cooker

Cooking root vegetables such as potatoes and carrots for longer than meat requires them to be chopped into smaller, even-sized pieces and placed on the bottom edges of the cooker, with the meat placed on the top. During the final 15 to 60 minutes of cooking, add additional delicate veggies. To conclude the cooking process, adding spinach, tomatoes, zucchini, basil, kale, peas, and parsley is preferable. To maintain the form of the dish while it is warming, canned beans are suggested and may be added during the final 30 minutes of cooking.

You may also use dry beans, although they are more difficult to prepare. If you're using dry beans, you must soak them overnight. When cooking dry beans, avoid adding acids, sugar, or salt at the beginning of the cooking process since this will prevent the beans from getting soft. Those Ingredients should be added at the end.

For dairy products, add milk, cream cheese, cheese, sour cream, and other dairy products to conclude cooking since they tend to break down over a longer period. Add eggs at the end of cooking. Fish and seafood should be added towards the end of the cooking process since they cook extremely fast. If you have roasts larger than 3 pounds, split them in half to ensure uniform cooking. Excess fat should be removed from the dish since it absorbs heat and may lead to overcooking. The option of browning certain meats before cooking may enhance the proteins' color and texture, but it is not required.

Instant oats work just as well as old-fashioned oats in a slow cooker, although old oats are preferable. Pasta should be cooked separately and then added at the end of the cooking process since dried pasta becomes extremely sticky in the slow cooker. Smaller pasta shapes, such as orzo, cook better in the slow cooker, but just until the final hour or so to avoid getting mushy and gummy. Instant rice should be added to the pot in the final 30 minutes of cooking time. Converted rice is an excellent choice for all-day cooking. It is important to skim off any extra fat from stews, braises, and chili before serving them. This lowers the fat level of the recipe while simultaneously making the meal more pleasant for the consumer. The fat may be removed using a big spoon, or the liquid can be poured into a fat separator and left for several hours until the fat rises to the top of the liquid.

1.9 Slow Cooker Safety

Although slow cookers are intended to cook for many hours and adequately heat food, you still need to follow basic safety measures.

- Never fill the stoneware container more than two-thirds of the way with water. Keep the lid on the container during the cooking procedure to ensure optimum cooking conditions throughout the cooking process.
- Ensure that you test the cooker regularly to ensure that it is heating properly and capable of cooking food to the appropriate serving temperature.
- To prevent bacteria growth, food should be cooked to at least 140°F within 4 hours after preparation.
- Fill your slow cooker halfway to two-thirds of the way with water, cover it with a lid, and cook on the low setting for 8 hours to see how well it works. Then, before the water begins to cool, use a food thermometer to keep the temperature. If the temperature inside the slow cooker reaches 185°F, it is okay to use it.
- A lower temperature may suggest that the heating element isn't working properly, and thus the food isn't being cooked completely.

- The low wattage of a slow cooker makes it safe to leave home while it is cooking. Although the base heats up, the device is not intended to get so hot to the point where it may ignite a tabletop.
- If your slow cooker does not have a detachable insert, you may clean the interior with a soapy sponge and wipe away any spills with a paper towel.
- Extreme temperature fluctuations might cause the stoneware insert to break, so you should avoid freezing it or using it over direct heat, such as a cooktop, if at all possible.
- A hot crock should never be placed on a cold surface; instead, use a heated pad to protect the porcelain. In the same way, if the pot is still hot, avoid pouring cold water into the pot.
- Before putting meat and poultry in the slow cooker, make sure they are completely defrosted.
- Before serving, check the temperature of the dishes using a thermometer to ensure they are hot enough.
- When preparing recipes that call for beans, keep in mind that dried beans will not work in a slow cooker. Dry beans, particularly dried red kidney beans, contain a toxin known as Phytohemagglutinin, which may induce nausea, vomiting, diarrhea, and stomach discomfort in susceptible individuals. This toxin may be removed from dry beans by soaking and boiling them; however, the temperature in a slow cooker never reaches high enough to heat dry beans properly. Dry beans should be soaked for at least 12 hours before being rinsed and boiled for 10 minutes before using them in your recipe. Another risk-free alternative is to utilize canned beans cooked before being put into a canner.
- Culinary with a slow cooker should be used for cooking purposes only; it should never be used for reheating. It is best to keep leftovers in shallow containers and refrigerate them within two hours after the meal. To reheat food, use another cooking technique, such as a stovetop or microwave, to bring the temperature of the meal back up to 165°F.
- Please make certain that the temperature of the cooking liquid in your slow cooker is 185°F to guarantee that it is operating properly. If the temperature is too high, the meat may be overcooked, and if it is too low, the meal will be hazardous to consume. The temperature danger zone for optimum development of spoilage microorganisms is about 40 to 140°F, particularly if the temperature is maintained at this range for more than 3 to 4 hours. Check to see that a slow cooker is functioning properly.

CHAPTER 2:

Appetizers And Soups

1. Cordon Bleu Soup

Prep time: 40 minutes

Cook time: 3 hours

Servings: 9

Ingredients

- 4 tbsp of melted butter
- 1/4 tbsp of garlic powder
- 1/4 tbsp of pepper
- 5 cubed French bread
- 1 diced small onion
- 1 diced celery ribs
- 1 minced garlic clove
- 1/4 tbsp of salt and pepper
- 3 cans of chicken broth
- 1/3 cups of all-purpose flour
- 1/3 cups of water
- 1/3 cup of white wine
- 9 oz. of cubed cream cheese
- 1 cup shredded Swiss cheese
- 1/2 cup of shredded cheddar cheese
- 1/2 pound of diced rotisserie chicken
- 1 pound of deli ham

Instructions

To make croutons, first, preheat the oven to 707 °F. Add the first 5 ingredients into the large bowl. Coat the bread crumbs. Let them get golden brown from all sides in 10 to 15mins by stirring every 5 minutes. After that, cool it for 5 minutes. In the slow cooker, combine the next 5 ingredients and cook on low for 2 hours. Increase heat to high and start adding other ingredients one by one in order with constant stirring. When thickened, serve with croutons at the end.

Nutrients: Kcal: 384, Fat, 20g, Total Carbs: 12g, Protein: 29g

2. Cheesy Potato Soup

Prep time: 20 minutes

Cook time: 4 hours

Servings: 10

Ingredients

- 14 1/2 ounces of diced potatoes
- 10 3/4 ounces of mushroom soup
- 2 1/2 cups of water
- 11 oz. of whole corn
- 10 oz. of diced tomatoes and green chilies
- 6 chopped green onions
- 1 chopped sweet red pepper
- 1 tbsp of dried minced onion
- 1 tbsp of cayenne pepper
- 1/4 tbsp of pepper
- 1 pound of pork sausage
- 8 oz. of shredded cheddar cheese
- 8 oz. of French onion dips
- Tortilla chips as required for serving

Instructions

Brown the sausages in a skillet for 8 minutes and add them to the slow cooker in the form of crumbs. Add the first 10 ingredients into the slow cooker. Cook on low for 5 hours. Now add the other ingredients into the slow cooker and cook for more than 30 to 1 hour with constant stirring. Serve with tortilla chips and enjoy!

Nutrients: Kcal: 400, Fat: 25, Total Carbs: 33, Protein: 18

3. Pumpkin Sausage Soup

Prep time: 20 minutes

Cook time: 3 hours 15 minutes

Servings: 8

Ingredients

- 1 pound of pork sausage
- 1/3 cup of chopped onion
- 14 1/2 oz. of chicken broth
- 15 oz. of pumpkin
- 1/2 cup of maple syrup
- 1 tsp of pumpkin pie spice
- 1/2 tsp of garlic powder
- 1/4 tsp of grounded nutmeg
- 12 ounces of evaporated milk

Instructions

Cook sausages and onion in a skillet until brown. Add them to the slow cooker along with the other ingredients except for milk. Add milk at the end and blend along. Serve with crackers if desired, and enjoy!

Nutrients: Kcal: 250, Fat: 14, Total Carbs: 24, Protein: 8

4. Bean Soup with Spinach

Prep time: 20 minutes

Cook time: 7 hours

Servings: 5

Ingredients

- 1 pound of dried navy beans
- 64 oz. of chicken broth
- 2 cups of water
- 7 oz. of smoked turkey wing
- 1 chopped onion
- 1 finely chopped jalapeno pepper
- 1 tbsp of minced garlic
- 4 bay leaves
- 1 tsp of pepper
- 1/2 tsp of crushed red pepper
- 10 cups of chopped fresh spinach
- 1 chopped large sweet red pepper
- 1/2 tsp of salt

Instructions

Rinse and soak beans accordingly and then add in the slow cooker with all other ingredients and cook on low until tender. Discard turkey wings and bay leaves. Serve hot with parmesan grated cheese and enjoy!

Nutrients: Kcal: 230, Fat: 2g, Total Carbs: 40, Protein: 15g

5. Butternut Squash Soup

Prep time: 25 minutes

Cook time: 5 hours

Servings: 12

Ingredients

- 3 pounds of peeled butternut squash
- 4 cups of water
- 32 oz. of chicken broth
- 3/4 cup of barley
- 2 of the chopped carrots
- 2 chopped celery ribs
- 1 chopped onion
- 2 tbsp of minced fresh parsley
- 2 minced garlic cloves
- 1 tsp of rubbed sage
- 1 1/4 tsp of salt
- 1/2 tsp of curry powder
- 1/4 tsp of pepper
- 2 cups of cubed cooked turkey

Instructions

Add all the ingredients into the slow cooker except for turkey and cook on low for 7 hours until tender. Stir in the turkey and cook for more than 15 minutes with the lid covered. Serve and enjoy!

Nutrients: Kcal: 120, Fat: 1g, Total Carbs: 23, Protein: 7g

6. Pork Bean Soup

Prep time: 20 minutes

Cook time: 7 hours

Servings: 12

Ingredients

- 16 ounces of any beans
- 1 chopped sweet onion
- 3 chopped carrots
- 3 chopped celery ribs
- 1 pound pork tenderloin
- 1 tsp of garlic powder
- 1 tbsp of fresh minced chives, oregano, thyme and pepper
- 32 ounces chicken broth
- 14 and 1/2 oz. of diced tomatoes
- 5 oz. of fresh spinach
- 2 tsp of salt

Instructions

Take overnight soaked beans, add them to a slow cooker and other ingredients and cook on low for 8 hours until tender. Now shred the pork with a fork and cook on low for 20 more minutes. Serve and enjoy!

Nutrients: Kcal: 201, Fat: 2g, Total Carbs: 30g, Protein: 18g

7. Pumpkin Soup

Prep time: 20 minutes

Cook time: 6 hours

Servings: 8

Ingredients

- 2 1/2 cups of water
- 15 ounces of pumpkin
- 2 quartered tomatoes
- 1 peeled and diced potatoes
- 1 chopped onion
- 3 tsp of spoons curry powder
- 2 tsp of chicken bouillon granules
- 1/2 tsp of salt
- 1/8 tsp of cayenne pepper
- 1/8 tsp of pepper
- 1 cup of milk
- 1/2 cup of heavy whipped cream

Instructions

Add in the first 10 ingredients and cook on low for 6 hours until tender. Then blend the material using a blender until smooth. Stir in milk and cook on high for more than 30 minutes. Serve and enjoy!

Nutrients: Kcal: 121, Fat: 7g, Total Carbs: 13g, Protein: 3g

8. Potato And Cheddar Creamy Soup

Prep time: 25 minutes

Cook time: 7 hours

Servings: 12

Ingredients

- 9 peeled and cubed potatoes
- 1 chopped red onion
- 1 chopped celery rib
- 28 oz. of chicken broth
- 10 oz. of condensed cream of celery soup
- 1 tsp of garlic powder
- 1/2 tsp of white pepper
- 1 cup of shredded sharp cheddar cheese
- 1 cup of half and half cream
- Shredded cheddar cheese

Instructions

Combine the first 7 ingredients in the slow cooker and heat on low for 7 hours until potatoes tender. Add and stir cream and cheese. Cook for more than 30 minutes until the cheese melts. Top with your choice and serve!

Nutrients: Kcal: 212, Fat: 8g, Total Carbs: 28g, Protein: 8g

9. Pumpkin And Black Bean Soup

Prep time: 20 minutes

Cook time: 4 hours

Servings: 10

Ingredients

- 2 tbsp of olive oil
- 1 chopped onion
- 1 chopped sweet yellow pepper
- 3 minced garlic cloves
- 30 oz. of black beans
- 15 oz. of pumpkin
- 14 1/2 oz. of diced tomatoes
- 3 cups of chicken broth
- 2 and 1/2 cups of cubed cooked turkey
- 2 tsp of dried parsley
- 2 tsp of chili powder
- 1 1/2 tsp of ground cumin
- Salt as desired

Instructions

Add onions, pepper and garlic into the skillet and cook until tender. Now add the rest of the ingredients into the slow cooker and cook on low flame for about 4 hours. Top it off with green onions and serve!

Nutrients: Kcal: 192, Fat: 5g, Total Carbs: 21g, Protein: 16g

10. Lentil Soup

Prep time: 20 minutes

Cook time: 5 hours

Servings: 12

Ingredients

- 4 cups of water and vegetable broth each
- 2 cups of dried lentils
- 3 chopped onions
- 1 chopped celery ribs
- 1 tsp of dried oregano
- 1 cup of chopped spinach
- 1/2 cup of tomato sauce
- 2 1/4 oz. of sliced olives
- 3 tbsp of red wine vinegar
- 2 minced garlic cloves
- 1/2 tsp of salt and pepper each

Instructions

Add in all the ingredients starting from the main ingredients at the top and cook on low for 5 hours until lentils are tender and spinach is wilted. Serve with lemon wedges and enjoy!

Nutrients: Kcal: 134, Fat: 1g, Total Carbs: 12, Protein: 9g

11. Lime Chicken Soup With Rice

Prep time: 35 minutes

Cook time: 4 hours

Servings: 12

Ingredients

- 2 tbsp of olive oil
- 2 pounds of boneless and skinless chicken breasts
- 14 1/2 oz. of chicken broth
- 8 cups of coarsely chopped kale
- 2 finely chopped carrots
- 1 chopped onion
- 1 thinly sliced lemon
- 1/4 cup of lemon juice
- 4 tsp of grated lemon zest
- 1/2 tsp of pepper
- 4 cups of cooked brown rice

Instructions

Cook the chicken in skillet till it's brown and transfer it into the slow cooker with the other ingredients. Cook on low heat with a covered lid for about 5 hours or until the chicken is tender. Add in rice as desired, and heat for more than serve and enjoy!

Nutrients: Kcal: 203, Fat: 5g, Total Carbs: 20g, Protein: 20g

12. Shrimp Chowder

Prep time: 15 minutes

Cook time: 3 hours

Servings: 12

Ingredients

- 1/2 cup of chopped onion
- 2 tsp of butter
- 24 oz. of evaporated milk
- 23 oz. of potato soup and chicken soup cream
- 7 oz. of white corn
- 1 tsp of seasoning
- 1/2 tsp of garlic powder
- 2 pounds of peeled and deveined cooked small shrimps
- 3 ounces of cubed cream cheese

Instructions

Brown the onion in skillet and then add in the slow cooker along with the other ingredients and stir in cheese and shrimps. Keep on heating until shrimps are tender and heated while cheese is melted.

Nutrients: Kcal: 202, Fat: 8g, Total Carbs: 13g, Protein: 20g

13. Vegetable Soup With Wild Rice

Prep time: 25 minutes

Cook time: 5 hours

Servings: 12

Ingredients

- 6 cups of vegetable broth
- 24 oz. of roasted and diced tomatoes
- 2 chopped celery ribs
- 2 chopped carrots
- 1 3/4 cups sliced mushrooms
- 1 chopped onion
- 1 peeled and cubed sweet potato
- 1 chopped green pepper
- 1 cup uncooked wild rice
- 2 minced garlic cloves
- 3/4 tsp of salt
- 1/4 tsp of pepper
- 3 bay leaves

Instructions

Add all the ingredients into the slow cooker and heat on low for 5 hours or until tender. Discard bay leaves before serving.

Nutrients: Kcal: 117, Fat: 0g, Total Carbs: 25g, Protein: 4g

14. Chicken Tomato Chili Soup

Prep time: 20 minutes

Cook time: 4 hours

Servings: 8

Ingredients

- 29 oz. of chicken broth
- 3 cups of cubed and cooked chicken
- 2 cups of frozen corn
- 10 oz. of tomato puree
- 10 oz. of diced tomatoes and green chilies
- 1 finely chopped onion
- 2 minced garlic cloves
- 1 bay leaf
- 2 tsp of ground cumin
- 1/2 tsp of salt and chili powder
- 1/8 tsp of pepper
- 1/8 tsp of pepper
- 4 yellow corn tortillas

Instructions

Add all the ingredients into the slow cooker and cover the lid. Heat on low for about 4 hours. Add in tortillas and serve!

Nutrients: Kcal: 196, Fat: 5g, Total Carbs: 19g, Protein: 19g

15. Cabbage Soup

Prep time: 15 minutes

Cook time: 6 hours

Servings: 10

Ingredients

- 4 cups of vegetable stock
- 14 oz. of diced tomatoes
- 6 oz. of tomato paste
- 1 1/2 pound of shredded cabbage
- 4 chopped celery ribs
- 2 chopped carrots
- 1 chopped onion
- 2 minced garlic cloves
- 2 tsp of Italian seasoning
- 1/2 tsp of salt

Instructions

Add all the ingredients into the slow cooker and cook on low for 6 hours. Serve and enjoy!

Nutrients: Kcal: 110, Fat: 0g, Total Carbs: 24g, Protein: 4g

16. Chicken Meatballs With Mozzarella Stuffing

Prep time: 20 minutes

Cook time: 6 hours

Servings: 5

Ingredients

For Sauce

- 28 oz. of crushed tomatoes
- 1/2 grated onion
- 1/4 cup of dry red wine
- 2 tbsp of tomato paste
- 2 minced garlic cloves
- 1/2 tsp of dried basil and oregano each
- 1/4 tsp of salt

For Meatballs

- 1 pound of ground chicken
- 1 lightly beaten egg
- 1 cup of grated parmesan cheese
- 1 cup of panko breadcrumbs
- 1/2 tsp of dried basil, oregano, garlic powder and salt each
- 8 oz. of small cubed mozzarella
- 16 oz. of cooked spaghetti

Instructions

Add all the ingredients required for the sauce in the slow cooker and make the meatball mixture in a medium bowl. Now Make meatballs stuffed with cheese in them and carefully place them inside the slow cooker. Cook on low for 6 hours and then serve hot with pasta.

Nutrients: Kcal: 570, Fats: 30g, Total Carbs: 50g, Protein: 33g

17. Cheese Queso

Prep time: 10 minutes

Cook time: 1 hour 30 minutes

Servings: 12

Ingredients

- 1 pound of shredded cheddar cheese
- 8 oz. of American cheese, shredded
- 3 tbsp of cornstarch
- 12 oz. of evaporated milk
- 1 tsp of garlic powder
- 1 tsp of onion powder
- 1 tsp of ground cumin
- 1 tsp of salt
- 7 oz. diced green chilies
- 2 of minced jalapenos

Instructions

Add all the ingredients into the slow cooker and cook on low for 1 hour and 30 minutes until all the cheese has melted. Serve hot and enjoy!

Nutrients: Kcal: 400, Fats: 45g, Total Carbs: 50g, Protein: 22g

18. Mini BBQ Smoky

Prep time: 10 minutes

Cook time: 2 hours

Servings: 10

Ingredients

- 2 cups of tomato ketchup
- 2 tbsp of liquid smoke
- 1 1/2 cups of brown sugar
- 1/2 cup of minced onion
- 2 of 13 ounces of packs of mini-BBQ smoky

Instructions

Add all the ingredients into the slow cooker and cook on high for 2 hours. Serve hot and enjoy!

Nutrients: Kcal: 450, Fats: 40g, Total Carbs: 34g, Protein: 35g

19. Honey Glazed Chipotle Meatballs

Prep time: 12 minutes

Cook time: 3 hours

Servings: 14

Ingredients

For Meatballs

- 2 pounds of ground chicken
- 1 cup of panko breadcrumbs
- 2 eggs
- 2 tbsp of grated parmesan cheese
- 1 tsp each of garlic powder and onion powder
- 1 1/2 tsp of salt
- 1/2 tsp of pepper

For Sauce

- 13 oz. of preserved cherry
- 18 oz. of honey glazed chipotle barbecue sauce
- 1/2 tsp of red pepper flakes and garlic powder

Instructions

Pour the sauce ingredients into the slow cooker and mix well. Then add the meatballs to the slow cooker and cover the lid. Cook on low for 2 hours. Stir after the first hour. And serve with green onion garnish.

Nutrients: Kcal: 330, Fats: 16g, Total Carbs: 23g, Protein: 33g

20. Bacon Dip Chicken Ranch

Prep time: 20 minutes

Cook time: 2 hours

Servings: 8

Ingredients

- 18 oz. of tortilla chips
- 2 pounds of the boneless and skinless chicken breast
- 15 oz. of the cream cheese
- 1 1/2 cup of the shredded chicken
- 1 cup of chicken broth
- 2 oz. of ranch seasoning
- 3 tbsp of hot sauce

Instructions

Add all the ingredients into the slow cooker and cook on high for 2 hours. After that, take out the chicken and shred it with a fork. Add back into the slow cooker and combine with the rest of the ingredients. Serve and enjoy!

Nutrients: Kcal: 450, Fats: 33g, Total Carbs: 6g, Protein: 33g

21. Cheese Sauce Salsa

Prep time: 20 minutes

Cook time: 5 hours

Servings: 12

Ingredients

- 1 cup of peeled and diced russet potatoes
- 1 cup of diced carrots
- 1/2 cup of chicken stock
- 1 tsp of salt
- 1/4 cup of raw cashews
- 1 tbsp of nutritional yeast
- 1 tbsp of olive oil
- 2 tsp of fresh lemon juice
- 1 peeled garlic clove not minced
- 1/4 cup of salsa

Instructions

Place potatoes, salt, carrots and stock in the slow cooker. Cook on low for 5 hours. Using the blender, add the rest of the ingredients into it and then carefully take it out in a bowl and mix with the slow cooker ingredients. Serve and enjoy!

Nutrients: Kcal: 200, Fats: 23, Total Carbs: 12, Protein: 23

22. Mixed Nut Ranch

Prep time: 3 minutes

Cook time: 2 hours

Servings: 5

Ingredients

- 20 oz. of salted nuts mix
- 1/2 cup of melted and salted butter
- 1.5 oz. of original ranch mix

Instructions

Add all the nuts into the slow cooker and whisk in the butter and ranch seasoning. Cover and cook on low for 2 hours and serve!

Nutrients: Kcal: 100, Fats: 45, Total Carbs: 12, Protein: 12

23. Mixed Nutty Snack

Prep time: 6 minutes

Cook time: 2 hours

Servings: 13

Ingredients

- 5 cups of each corn and wheat square-shaped cereal
- 5 cups of small pretzel twists
- 3 cups of cheddar cheese with fish-shaped crackers
- 6 oz. of Blue Diamond Almonds
- 1 cup of melted butter
- 5 tsp of any desired seasoning mix

Instructions

Add all the ingredients into the slow cooker and mix well. Cook on high for 2 hours. Cool before serving and enjoy!

Nutrients: Kcal: 200, Fats: 45g, Total Carbs: 50g, Protein: 37g

24. Lettuce And Beefy Wrap

Prep time: 10 minutes

Cook time: 20 minutes

Servings: 10

Ingredients

- 5 pounds of boneless roasted beef chuck
- 3/4 cup of beef stock
- 1/2 cup of soy sauce
- 2 tbsp of sweet chili sauce
- 2 tbsp of honey
- 2 tsp of minced ginger
- 2 minced garlic cloves
- 2 tsp of sesame oil
- 2 tsp of red pepper flakes
- 1 tbsp of cornstarch
- 2 tbsp of water
- lettuce
- Shredded carrots and cucumber

Instructions

Add all the ingredients required for making the beef roast in a slow cooker and cook on low for 10 hours. Once tender, add the water and cornstarch mixture into the slow cooker and cook for more than 30 minutes. Serve with beef and salad wrapped in lettuce, and enjoy!

Nutrients: Kcal: 350, Fats: 20g, Total Carbs: 40g, Protein: 70g

25. Sour And Sweet Chicken Wings

Prep time: 20 minutes

Cook time: 4 hours

Servings: 8

Ingredients

- 1 peeled and chopped ginger
- Peeled and chopped 4 garlic cloves
- 3/4 cup of brown sugar
- 1/4 cup of soy sauce
- 2 tsp of Sriracha sauce
- 1/4 tsp of cayenne pepper
- 5 pounds of chicken wings
- 1/4 cup of water
- 1/4 cup of tomato paste

Instructions

Add all the ingredients into the slow cooker except for the water, tomato paste and half cup of brown sugar, soy sauce and pepper. Cook for 2 hours on low. In a medium bowl, whisk together the left ingredients and occasionally coat the wings while keeping the wings cooking. In the end, serve and enjoy!

Nutrients: Kcal: 473, Fats: 30g, Total Carbs: 55g, Protein: 45g

CHAPTER 3:

Meat Meals

1. Pulled BBQ Chicken

Prep time: 5 minutes

Cook time: 6 hours 30 minutes

Servings: 8

Ingredients

- 4 boneless chicken breast fillets
- 8.5 fl oz of ketchup
- 2 tbsp of Worcestershire sauce
- 1/2 tsp of chili powder
- 1/8 tsp of cayenne pepper
- 1/2 tsp of barbecue sauce
- 2 tbsp of mustard
- 2 tsp of lemon juice
- 1/4 tsp of garlic
- 14.2 fl oz of maple syrup
- 8 rolls

Instructions

Add the chicken breasts to the slow cooker. Mix ketchup, mustard, lemon juice, garlic granules, maple syrup, barbecue sauce, chili powder, cayenne pepper, and hot sauce in a mixing bowl until combined. Pour the sauce over the chicken and cook for about 6 hours on low in the slow cooker. Cook for another 30 minutes after shredding the chicken. Spoon the chicken and sauce into the sandwich rolls and serve.

Nutrients: Kcal 223, Fat: 1.5g, Total Carbs: 23.1g, Protein: 27.8g

2. Simple Chicken Casserole

Prep time: 10 minutes

Cook time: 4 hours

Servings: 4

Ingredients

- 4 chicken thighs
- 4 carrots
- 4 bay leaves
- 2 potatoes
- 1 onion
- 4 tsp of garlic
- 1 tsp of parsley
- 1.4 oz of pearl barley
- 0.7 oz of peas
- 0.7 oz of fat peas
- 20.1fl oz of chicken stock
- salt and pepper to taste

Instructions

Take chopped carrots, onion, and garlic, simmer for about 5 minutes in a medium heated skillet, add diced potatoes and herbs and cook for another 5 minutes. Toss everything into the slow cooker. In a frying pan, brown the chicken for about 5 minutes. Toss it in the slow cooker. Further combine the bay leaves, salt and pepper, barley, split peas, marrowfat peas, and stock. Cook for about 3-4 hours on high or 8 hours on low. Serve with roast potatoes, stuffing, or buttered toast.

Nutrients: Kcal 296, Fat: 26g, Total Carbs: 23g, Protein: 18g

3. Delicious Baked Chicken

Prep time: 20 minutes

Cook time: 10 hours

Servings: 6

Ingredients

- 1 whole chicken
- 1 tsp of paprika
- salt to taste
- pepper to taste

Instructions

Form three pieces of aluminum foil and set them in the slow cooker's bottom. Marinate the chicken with salt, pepper, and paprika, then set it on the crushed aluminum foil balls in the slow cooker. Set the slow cooker too high for about 1 hour, then low for about 8 to 10 hours, or until the chicken is no longer pink and the juices flow clear.

Nutrients: Kcal 321.3, Fat: 7.1g, Total Carbs: 28.4g, Protein: 35.9g

4. Creamy Chicken with Mushroom Sauce

Prep time: 10 minutes

Cook time: 8 hours

Servings: 6

Ingredients

- 6 chicken breast fillets
- 4 tbsp of plain flour
- salt to taste
- pepper to taste
- paprika to taste
- 4.1 fl oz of white wine
- 10.4 fl oz of mushroom soup
- 3.5 oz of mushrooms
- 8.5 fl oz of soured cream

Instructions

Season the chicken breasts to taste with salt, pepper, and paprika. Put everything in the slow cooker. Combine the wine, soup, and mushrooms in a mixing bowl. Combine the soured cream and flour in a separate bowl. In a mixing bowl, combine the cream, mushrooms, and wine. Pour the sauce over the chicken in the slow cooker. Top with more paprika. Cook on low for about 6 to 8 hours, covered.

Nutrients: Kcal 688, Fat: 21.6g, Total Carbs: 69.4g, Protein: 55.7g

5. Garlic Honey Chicken

Prep time: 10 minutes

Cook time: 6 hours

Servings: 5

Ingredients

- 10 chicken thighs
- 8.6 fl oz of soya sauce
- 8.9 fl oz of tomato ketchup
- 6.3 fl oz of honey
- 6 tsp of garlic
- 1 tsp of dried basil

Instructions

Add the chicken breasts to the slow cooker. Mix ketchup, mustard, lemon juice, garlic granules, maple syrup, barbecue sauce, chili powder, cayenne pepper, and hot sauce in a mixing bowl until combined. Pour the sauce over the chicken and cook for about 6 hours on low in the slow cooker. Cook for another 30 minutes after shredding the chicken. Spoon the chicken and sauce into the sandwich rolls and serve.

Nutrients: Kcal 255, Fat: 3.1g, Total Carbs: 40.8g, Protein: 19.6g

6. Lamb Shanks With Burgundy Sauce

Prep time: 15 minutes

Cook time: 8 hours

Servings: 4

Ingredients

- 4 lamb shanks
- 2 tbsp of parsley
- 2 tsp of garlic
- 1/2 tsp of oregano
- 1/2 tsp of lemon zest
- 2.6 oz of onion
- 1 Carrot
- 1 tsp of olive oil
- 8.8 fl oz of Burgundy wine
- 1 tsp of beef stock
- salt to taste
- pepper to taste

Instructions

Sauté the onion and carrot in oil in a small pot for about 3-4 minutes, or until soft. Combine the wine and beef stock. Bring the mixture to a boil, stirring regularly. Put the lamb in a slow cooker. Season the lamb with salt and pepper along with parsley, garlic, oregano, and lemon zest. Pour over the mixture the lamb. Cook on low for 8 hours, or until the meat is soft. Remove the lamb and keep it warm. Bring juices to a boil in a small saucepan; simmer until liquid is reduced by half. Serve alongside lamb.

Nutrients: Kcal 585, Fat: 24g, Total Carbs: 18g, Protein: 71g

7. Tender Lamb With Tomato Stew

Prep time: 10 minutes

Cook time: 7 hours

Servings: 2

Ingredients

- 2 onions
- 1 tbsp of olive oil
- 12.3 oz of lamb
- 1 tsp of garlic
- 3 tomatoes
- 1 tbsp of tomato puree
- salt to taste
- pepper to taste
- 1 tsp of white wine
- 1 tsp of dried oregano
- 1/2 tsp of paprika
- 8.8 fl oz of lamb stock

Instructions

Set the slow cooker on low heat. Transfer the onions to the slow cooker after frying them in olive oil until they are slightly transparent. Combine all of the other Ingredients. Put the cover on and leave it for about 7 to 8 hours. Remove the cover about 1-2 hours before serving to thicken the sauce.

Nutrients: Kcal 369, Fat: 16.4g, Total Carbs: 30.5g, Protein: 27.2 g

8. Mint lamb with Mashed Potatoes

Prep time: 10 minutes

Cook time: 6 hours

Servings: 5

Ingredients

- 1 tbsp of oil
- 1 onion, chopped
- 1 pound of lamb mince
- 1 carrot, sliced
- 5 mushrooms, sliced
- 1 tsp of mint sauce
- 1 small handful of plain flour
- 1 hot lamb stock
- salt and pepper

Instructions

In a large skillet, heat the oil, fry the onion until tender but not browned, and add the lamb and cook until browned. Stir in the carrot, mushrooms, and mint sauce. Sprinkle with flour, then add the stock and mix thoroughly. Season with salt and pepper to taste. Cook for about 15–20 minutes. Transfer to a slow cooker, cover, and cook on low for about 8 hours. Serve with mashed potatoes.

Nutrients: Kcal 253, Fat: 23.5g, Total Carbs: 3.63g, Protein: 6.18g

9. Lamb Shoulder With Mint Gravy

Prep time: 5 minutes

Cook time: 8 hours

Servings: 4

Ingredients

- 35.2 oz of lamb shoulder
- 7.6 fl oz of lamb stock
- 6.7 fl oz of red wine
- 1 tsp of mixed herbs
- black pepper to taste
- 1 tsp of corn flour
- 1 tsp of redcurrant jelly
- mint sauce

Instructions

Set the slow cooker on low heat. In the pot, place the lamb. Pour the stock and wine over the top. Season with dry herbs and pepper to taste. Cover with a lid and stir. Cook for about 7 to 8 hours on low, tossing and flipping lamb regularly. Remove the lamb from the slow cooker and keep warm for about 20 minutes before serving. Stir in the corn flour, and mint sauce leave the lid off the cooker. Increase the heat to high to thicken the gravy slightly. Carve or pull apart the meat. Pour the gravy over the lamb and stir in the redcurrant jelly. Serve

Nutrients: Kcal 412, Fat: 20g, Total Carbs: 5g, Protein: 44g

10. Lamb Shanks With Rosemary

Prep time: 20 minutes

Cook time: 8 hours

Servings: 2

Ingredients

- 2 lamb shanks
- 2 tbsp of olive oil
- 12 shallots
- 3 tsp of garlic
- 1 tsp of rosemary
- salt to taste
- pepper to taste
- 2 tbsp of plain flour
- 1.9 oz of butter
- 3 carrots
- 2 sticks celery
- 4 potatoes
- 14.1 oz of tomatoes
- 17 fl oz of red wine
- 10 fl oz of vegetable stock
- 2 tbsp of parsley

Instructions

Preheat the slow cooker to low. Heat the oil in a frying pan and add the shallots. Cook for about 6 minutes, till they are brown. Add garlic and rosemary. Season the lamb shanks well with salt and pepper, then coat with flour and place in the slow cooker. Melt the butter in the same frying pan and add the shanks, browning evenly on both sides for about 6 to 8 minutes. Combine the carrots, celery, potatoes, and tomatoes in a mixing bowl. Cook for 3 minutes and add the red wine and vegetable stock, bringing to a boil. Transfer to the slow cooker and cook on low for about 7 to 8 hours. Serve with fresh chopped parsley on top.

Nutrients: Kcal 585, Fat: 19g, Total Carbs: 25g, Protein: 72g

11. Pork Fillet

Prep time: 15 minutes

Cook time: 4 hours

Servings: 6

Ingredients

- 31.7 oz of pork fillet
- 1.4 oz of onion soup mix
- 8.5 fl oz of water
- 8.1 fl oz of red wine
- 3 tbsp of garlic
- 3 tbsp of soy sauce
- black pepper to taste

Instructions

Place the pork fillet in a slow cooker with the soup mix. Pour the water, wine, and soy sauce over the meat and flip to coat. Spread the garlic evenly over the pork, leaving as much on top as possible throughout cooking. Season with pepper, cover, and simmer on low for about 4 hours. Serve.

Nutrients: Kcal 180, Fat: 3g, Total Carbs: 5g, Protein: 24g

12. Ham With Maple Syrup

Prep time: 15 minutes

Cook time: 10 hours

Servings: 12

Ingredients

- 45.8 oz of gammon joint
- 25.4 fl oz of cloudy apple juice
- 7.1 oz of brown sugar
- 7.6 fl oz of maple syrup
- 2 tbsp of cinnamon
- 1 tbsp of nutmeg
- 2 tsp of ginger
- 2 tbsp of ground cloves
- 1 tbsp of vanilla extract
- 1 orange

Instructions

In a slow cooker, place the ham. Pour in some apple juice until the ham is barely above the surface. Massage the brown sugar into the cloves on top of the ham. Over the ham, pour the maple syrup, cinnamon, nutmeg, ginger, ground cloves, and vanilla. Toss in the orange peel with the rest of the Ingredients in the saucepan. Fill the slow cooker with as much apple juice as you can. Cover at low for about 8 to 10 hours. Serve when done.

Nutrients: Kcal 150, Fat: 7g, Total Carbs: 2g, Protein: 0.1g

13. Pork And Apple Casserole

Prep time: 20 minutes

Cook time: 8 hours

Servings: 4

Ingredients

- 4 pork chops
- 3 apples
- 2 onions
- 1 tsp of sage leaves
- 17 fl oz of cider
- 2 tsp of wholegrain mustard

Instructions

In your slow cooker, layer the onions, apples, and chops in that order. Between each layer and on top, scatter the chopped sage leaves. Mix in the mustard with the cider. Pour the cider over the Ingredients to coat them completely. Cook for about 8 hours on low in a slow cooker. Serve with veggies and a creamy mash.

Nutrients: Kcal 232, Fat: 8g, Total Carbs: 13g, Protein: 28g

14. Pork Chops With Veggies

Prep time: 10 minutes

Cook time: 8 hours

Servings: 2

Ingredients

- Cooking oil
- 2 pork chops
- 4 onions
- 1 tsp of garlic
- 1 tsp of sugar
- 6.8 fl oz of cider
- seasoning
- 4 tbsp of frozen petit pois
- 2 tbsp of butter

Instructions

Reduce the heat to low in the slow cooker. Heat some oil in a frying pan. Cook the pork chops until they are golden brown on both sides. Remove the chicken from the pan and place it in the slow cooker. Add the onions to the same pan and cook steadily until they are slightly caramelized. Stir in the garlic and the sugar for a few minutes. Bring to a boil with the cider. On top of the pork chops, pour the onion and cider mixture. Season to taste and cover. Add the peas 30 minutes before serving, stir well, and simmer for another 30 minutes. Remove the pork chops from the pan and set them on a bed of mashed potatoes to serve. Pour over a knob of butter mixed with the juices.

Nutrients: Kcal 509, Fat: 24.8g, Total Carbs: 36g, Protein: 35.5g

15. Roasted Pork

Prep time: 10 minutes

Cook time: 6 hours

Servings: 8

Ingredients

- 1 onion
- 35 oz of boneless pork loin roast
- 8.5 fl oz of hot water
- 4 tbsp of sugar
- 3 tbsp of red wine vinegar
- 2 tbsp of soy sauce
- 1 tbsp of ketchup
- 1/2 tsp of black pepper
- 1/2 tsp of salt
- 1/4 tsp of garlic granules
- 1 tsp of hot sauce

Instructions

Arrange onion slices equally over the bottom of the slow cooker, then set the roast on top. Pour water, sugar, vinegar, soy sauce, ketchup, black pepper, salt, garlic granules, and spicy sauce over the roast in a mixing bowl. Cook on low for about 6 to 8 hours or high for about 3 to 4 hours, covered. Serve when done.

Nutrients: Kcal 132, Fat: 4.4g, Total Carbs: 4.8g, Protein: 18.5g

16. Beef Lasagna

Prep time: 20 minutes

Cook time: 4 hours 20 minutes

Servings: 10

Ingredients

- 16 oz of beef
- 1 onion
- 2 tsp of garlic
- 27 fl oz of pasta
- 150g tomato puree
- 1 1/2 tsp of salt
- 1 tsp of oregano
- 12.3 oz of lasagna sheets
- 12.3 oz of cottage cheese
- 1.8 oz of Parmesan cheese
- 15.8 oz of mozzarella cheese

Instructions

Cook beef, onion, and garlic in a large frying skillet over medium heat until golden. Stir in the passata, tomato puree, salt, and oregano until completely combined. Cook until well heated. Combine the cottage cheese, grated Parmesan cheese, and grated mozzarella cheese in a large mixing basin. Pour a layer of the meat mixture into the slow cooker's bottom. Place two layers of uncooked lasagna sheets on top of each other. Place a dollop of the cheese mixture on top of the spaghetti. Layer the sauce, pasta sheets, and cheese until all of the Ingredients have been utilized. Cover and cook for about 4 to 6 hours on the low setting, then serve.

Nutrients: Kcal 388, Fat: 17.6g, Total Carbs: 43g, Protein: 27.1g

17. Beef Chili

Prep time: 15 minutes

Cook time: 6 hours

Servings: 16

Ingredients

- 1 1/4 pound of beef
- 1 onion
- 2 celeries
- 1 green pepper
- 2 tsp of garlic
- 21.1 oz of jar passata
- 28.2 oz of kidney beans
- 14.1 oz of cannellini beans
- 1/2 tbsp of chili powder
- 1/2 tsp of dried parsley
- 1 tsp of salt
- 3/4 tsp of dried basil
- 3/4 tsp of dried oregano
- 1/4 tsp of ground black pepper

Instructions

In the bottom of a slow cooker, layer half of the onion rings. On top of the onions, place the beef. Pour chopped tomatoes, beef stock and coffee over the roast in the cooker. Add diced green chilies, jalapeno peppers, garlic, chili powder, cumin, salt, and black pepper to taste. Over the mixture, scatter the remaining onion rings. Cook on low for about 6 to 10 hours. Place the beef in a large mixing basin and shred it with two forks. Toss the shredded beef back into the sauce. Remove the onions from the pan and place them on top of the steak in the tortillas.

Nutrients: Kcal 499.3, Fat: 31g, Total Carbs: 10.5g, Protein: 37.1g

18. Beef Dumplings And Stew

Prep time: 10 minutes

Cook time: 10 hours

Servings: 4

Ingredients

- 4 carrots
- 2 onions
- 8 potatoes
- 4 tbsp of frozen peas
- 1.4 oz of dried pearl barley
- 1 pound of stewing beef.
- 1 tsp of marmite
- 2 tbsp of Worcestershire sauce
- 1.3 oz of gravy granules
- 1.8 oz of suet
- 3.5 oz of flour
- salt to taste
- pepper to taste

Instructions

After chopping the first six Ingredients, place them in the slow cooker immediately. Fill the container halfway with water. Stir in the Marmite, Worcestershire sauce, and gravy granules until everything is well combined. Cook on low for the entire day or on high for about 5-6 hours. In a mixing basin, combine suet, flour, salt, and pepper; gradually add water, constantly stirring, until the mixture. Continue to cook dumplings on a high in the slow cooker for about 30 minutes. Divide into 4 balls and set on top of the broth. Serve the stew.

Nutrients: Kcal 360, Fat: 7g, Total Carbs: 29.9g, Protein: 43.1g

19. Beef Casserole with Red wine

Prep time: 20 minutes

Cook time: 3 hours 15 minutes

Servings: 6

Ingredients

- 5 tbsp of flour
- salt to taste
- pepper to taste
- 35.2 oz of beef stewing steak
- 1 fl oz of olive oil
- 1 tbsp of spring onions
- 4 tbsp of garlic
- 17.6 oz of mushrooms
- 1 bottle of red wine
- 3 tbsp of tomato puree
- 1 beef stock cube
- 4 slices of bacon

Instructions

Combine the salt, pepper, and flour, and cover the meat in it. Place it in a large casserole dish and fry it in the oil for about 5 minutes or until golden. Preheat the slow cooker on low. Fry the onions for about 3 to 5 minutes in the oil, add the garlic for the final 2 minutes, then combine them with the meat. Quarter the mushrooms and add them to the casserole. Reheat the wine until it's barely boiling, and then whisk it in. Combine the tomato puree, bay leaf, beef stock, and bacon in a mixing bowl. Cover and cook for about 2 to 3 hours on low, then remove the lid and cook for another 1 hour Nutrients: Kcal 355, Fat: 11.8g, Total Carbs: 29g, Protein: 30.2g

20. Beef Braised Ribs

Prep time: 10 minutes

Cook time: 4 hours

Servings: 4

Ingredients

- 2 tbsp olive oil
- 1.2 kg beef short ribs
- 1 shallot
- 4 tsp of garlic
- 1 tsp of ginger
- 8.5 ml of sake
- 17 fl oz of beef stock
- 3.4 fl oz of soy sauce
- 3.4 fl oz of mirin
- 3.4 fl oz of wine vinegar
- 2 tbsp brown sugar

Instructions

In a large saucepan, heat the olive oil over high heat. Sear the ribs on all sides until brown, seasoning with a sprinkle of sea salt. Remove all except some oil from the pan and drain it. Cook for about 3 minutes until the shallot, garlic, and ginger are colored, then pour in the sake and cook for about 2 minutes. Move beef ribs to the slow cooker and add the additional Ingredients along with pan ones. C cook for about 3 to4 hours on low.

Nutrients: Kcal 664, Fat: 41.3g, Total Carbs: 15.8g, Protein: 44.7g

21. Tender Turkey With Herbs

Prep time: 15 minutes

Cook time: 6 hours

Servings: 6

Ingredients

- 88 oz of turkey crown
- salt to taste
- black pepper to taste
- 5 tsp of rosemary
- 5 tsp of thyme
- 1 onion
- 3.9 oz of butter
- 8.8 oz of celery leaves
- 12.7 fl oz of white wine

Instructions

Season the turkey crown with black pepper and salt. Place rosemary, thyme sprigs, onion and butter slices in the cavity of the turkey crown. In a slow cooker, combine the celery leaves, remaining onion and remaining herbs. With the top facing down, place the turkey crown on top of the veggies and herbs. Cover the white wine on the stove. Cook on high for about 6 hours. Remove the saucepan from the oven and cover with foil. Allow 15 minutes for the turkey breast to rest before slicing.

Nutrients: Kcal 150, Fat: 6g, Total Carbs: 2g, Protein: 20g

22. Turkey Casserole

Prep time: 10 minutes

Cook time: 8 hours

Servings: 2

Ingredients

- 1 turkey leg
- 1/2 celery
- 1/2 swede
- 1 sweet potato
- 17 fl oz of chicken stock

Instructions

In a slow cooker, combine the turkey, celeriac, swede, and sweet potato. Cover with a lid after adding the chicken stock. Cook for about 8 hours on medium or 10 hours on low.

Nutrients: Kcal 217, Fat: 5.93 g, Total Carbs: 16.8g, Protein: 23.5g

23. Hot Turkey Chili

Prep time: 15 minutes

Cook time: 2 hours 15 minutes

Servings: 10

Ingredients

- 1 tbsp of olive oil
- 24 oz of turkey mince
- 1 onion
- 2 tsp of garlic
- 4.1 fl oz of beer
- 1 tbsp of chili powder
- 2 tsp of salt
- 1 tsp of black pepper
- 28.2 oz of tomatoes
- 1 tbsp of green chilies
- 14.1 oz of kidney beans
- 1 tbsp of chili powder
- 1 tsp of ground black pepper
- 1 tsp of ground cayenne pepper
- 1/2 tsp of paprika
- 1/2 tsp of dried oregano
- 1/2 tsp of ground cumin
- 4.1 fl oz of chicken stock

Instructions

In a frying pan, heat the olive oil. Brown, the turkey mince in a large skillet, then add the onion and garlic. Cook, tossing regularly, for approximately 8 minutes. Add chili powder, salt, black pepper and stir to blend. Simmer for another 5 minutes. Pour in the beer and heat until it has reduced to roughly half its original volume. Combine the tomatoes, chilies, kidney beans, chili powder, black pepper, cayenne pepper, paprika, oregano, and cumin in a slow cooker. Add the turkey mixture and chicken stock and stir to combine. Cook for about 2 hours on high in the slow cooker.

Nutrients: Kcal 222 Fat: 3g, Total Carbs: 20g, Protein: 32g

24. Milky Turkey Stew

Prep time: 20 minutes

Cook time: 6 hours

Servings: 8

Ingredients

- 1 turkey breast fillet
- 5 red potatoes
- 3 carrots
- 3 sticks celery
- 21 fl oz of cream of chicken soup
- 2 tbsp of milk
- 4 tbsp of chicken stock
- 2 tsp of garlic, minced
- 1 tsp of sage
- 1 tsp of oregano
- pepper to taste
- 7.1 oz of frozen mixed vegetables

Instructions

In a slow cooker, combine all Ingredients and cook on high for about 5 hours. Cook for an additional hour after adding frozen mixed veggies to the slow cooker.

Nutrients: Kcal 180.6, Fat: 2.5g, Total Carbs: 15.8g, Protein: 23.5g

25. Turkey Delight

Prep time: 10 minutes

Cook time: 6 hours

Servings: 4

Ingredients

- 1 whole turkey
- 6 big carrots
- 15 mini onions
- 1 tbsp of coriander
- 8.3 fl oz of cranberry sauce
- 4.2 fl oz of vegetable stock
- 7.1 oz of basmati rice
- 17 fl oz of chicken stock

Instructions

Place the turkey on the bottom of the slow cooker. Cut and peel carrots, onions and coriander. Arrange them in a circle around the turkey. Cover with cranberry sauce and vegetable stock. Cook for about 6 hours. Using chicken stock, cook basmati rice. Serve the turkey with rice.

Nutrients: Kcal 63.3, Fat: 0.3g, Total Carbs: 2.9g, Protein: 11.2g

CHAPTER 4:

Fish Meals

1. Creamy Fish Chowder

Prep time: 30 minutes

Cook time: 4 hours

Servings: 9

Ingredients

- 5 ounces of halibut, cut into bite-size pieces
- 5 ounces of uncooked medium prawns, peeled and deveined
- 8 ounces of scallops
- 3 ounces of fresh or frozen sweetcorn
- 12 fl oz of cream
- 2 large potatoes, diced
- 3 stalks of celery, diced
- 2 large carrots, diced
- Freshly ground black pepper to taste
- 1/2 tsp of crushed chili flakes
- 50 ounces of stock
- 4 slices of chopped bacon
- 1 chopped onion
- 2 cloves of garlic, minced

Instructions

Grease a pan and cook bacon for 7-8 minutes until it gets brown. Add garlic and onion with bacon, cook for more than 5 minutes, till onion gets soft. Place the bacon mixture and stock, sweetcorn, potatoes, celery, and carrots in a slow cooker. Season with black pepper and crushed chili flakes, and cook for 3 hours on high. Add scallops, prawns and halibut into the slow cooker and cook for 1 more hour. Stir cream in chowder and serve.

Nutrients: Kcal 311, Fat: 13g, Total Carbs: 37g, Protein: 14g

2. Chickpeas With Fish Stew

Prep time: 10 minutes

Cook time: 1 hour

Servings: 4

Ingredients

- 4 oz of tomato passata
- 14 ounces of chickpeas, drained and rinsed
- 1 pound of white fish fillets
- 1 or 2 tbsp of oil
- 1/2 tsp of turmeric
- 1 onion, chopped
- 1/2 tsp of cumin
- 3 chopped tomatoes
- 2 tbsp of plain flour
- Freshly chopped parsley
- 3 cloves of garlic, crushed
- Salt and pepper to taste

Instructions

Add chopped onion to a slow cooker and cook for 15 minutes to soften. Add fish fillets and turn to coat in flour, salt, cumin, pepper and turmeric in a bowl. Settle fish slices on top of onion; add chickpeas, parsley, tomatoes, garlic and passata over it. Cook for 1 hour and serve.

Nutrients: Kcal 232, Fat: 4g, Total Carbs: 17g, Protein: 27g

3. Easy Clam Chowder

Prep time: 10 minutes

Cook time: 8 hours

Servings: 10

Ingredients

- 10 ounces of baby clams, drained
- 14 ounces of clam chowder
- 10 ounces of condensed cream of celery soup
- 10 ounces of condensed cream of chicken
- 50 fl oz of whipping cream
- 50 ounces of single cream
- 1-2 tsp of instant mash

Instructions

Add chicken soup, clam chowder, celery soup, clams, single cream, instant mash and whipping cream into a slow cooker and cover it with a lid. Cook for 6-8 hours on low. Serve and enjoy.

Nutrients: Kcal 156, Fat: 5.5g, Total Carbs: 20.8g, Protein: 6.6g

4. Easy Smoked Coley

Prep time: 10 minutes

Cook time: 2 hours

Servings: 4

Ingredients

- 1 tin of chopped tomatoes
- 10 ounces of white wine
- 2 smoked coley fillets
- 5 to 6 mushrooms, sliced
- 5 to 6 potatoes, peeled and cubed
- 1 onion, chopped
- 3 cloves of garlic, chopped
- 1 tbsp of olive oil
- Parsley, to taste

Instructions

Add onions, garlic and olive oil to a slow cooker. Add chopped tomatoes and water on top of it. Season with white wine and parsley. Finally, add the coley, sliced mushrooms and potatoes. Stir it and cook for 2 hours, until potatoes become soft. Serve with rice or simply in a bowl.

Nutrients: Kcal 500, Fat: 16g, Total Carbs: 59g, Protein: 47g

5. Delicious Thai Fish Curry

Prep time: 20 minutes

Cook time: 5 hours

Servings: 4

Ingredients

- 1pound of white fish, cubed
- 4 tsp of Thai green curry paste
- 40 ounces of thin coconut milk
- 20 ounces of vegetable stock, warmed
- 3 carrots, peeled and chopped
- Salt and pepper, to taste
- 3 spring onions, chopped
- 1 bunch of chopped fresh coriander
- 1 sprig Thai basil, leaves chopped
- 2 tbsp of sunflower oil
- 1/2 onion, chopped
- 1 green chili, seeded and finely chopped
- 1/4 of root ginger, chopped
- 1 tbsp of fish sauce
- 1 lime juice
- 1 pinch of ground nutmeg

Instructions

Heat the oil in a large casserole dish, then add the chopped onion, chili and root ginger. Stir and cook for 4 minutes until the onion gets soft. Add curry paste, fish sauce, lime juice and nutmeg in the mixture and cook for 2 minutes. Add coconut milk and stock, bring it to simmer and then add cubed fish and carrots. Transfer this mixture to a slow cooker and cook for 3 hours on high or 4-5 hours on low. Season with coriander or Thai basil before serving.

Nutrients: Kcal 322, Fat: 23g, Total Carbs: 11g, Protein: 21g

6. Jamaican Fish Stew

Prep time: 15 minutes

Cook time: 9 hours

Servings: 4

Ingredients

- 1 pound of red salmon
- 1 Scotch bonnet pepper
- 1 plantain
- 1 medium sweet potato
- 1 tin of black-eyed beans
- 1 medium onion
- 40 ounces of coconut milk
- 1/3 of butternut squash
- 1/2 tsp of red pepper
- 2 tsp of ground allspice
- 2 cloves of garlic
- 20 fl oz of stock

Instructions

Add diced potatoes to a slow cooker and pour stock on it until potatoes are well covered. Add drained black-eyed beans, chopped onion, butternut squash, red pepper and scotch bonnet pepper, minced garlic, red salmon, and sliced plantain and then pour on the coconut milk over it in a separate bowl. Add all the spices to the bowl and transfer this mixture to sweet potatoes. Cook for 9 hours, until water is absorbed and vegetables get tender.

Nutrients: Kcal 335, Fat: 21g, Total Carbs: 13g, Protein: 27g

7. Salmon With Rice

Prep time: 20 minutes

Cook time: 2 hours

Servings: 1

Ingredients

- 1 pound of salmon fillet
- 12 ounces of vegetable stock
- 2 ounces of rice
- 1 small onion, chopped
- 4 mushrooms, chopped
- 1/2 red pepper, chopped
- 1 tsp of margarine or butter
- 1 tsp of chili powder
- 1 tbsp of light soy sauce
- 1 tbsp of lime juice
- 1 garlic clove, crushed

Instructions

Sauté mushrooms, onion and red pepper in some butter in a pan. Put these in a slow cooker along with stock and chili powder, cook for 30 minutes on high. Place rice in the slow cooker and cook for 15 minutes. Mix the soy sauce, lime juice and garlic in a small bowl and lay the salmon in the sauce, top side down, and leave for 15 minutes. After marination, place the sauce of salmon in the slow cooker, lay salmon on top of rice, and cook for 1 hour on low.

Nutrients: Kcal 179, Fat: 5g, Total Carbs: 8g, Protein: 24g

8. Easy Fish Stew

Prep time: 15 minutes

Cook time: 2 hours 15 minutes

Servings: 6

Ingredients

- 1 pound of clams
- 13 oz of cod loin
- 12 oz of raw tiger prawns
- 1 tsp of rapeseed oil
- 1 onion, sliced
- 2 roasted red pepper
- 3 garlic cloves, finely sliced
- 1 tsp of grated fresh ginger
- 1 tsp of sweet smoked paprika
- 1/4 tsp of cayenne pepper
- 7 fl oz of white wine
- 2 tins of chopped tomatoes
- 1/2 of caster sugar
- 2 fresh bay leaves
- 1 pinch of saffron
- 1 lime juice
- A small handful of parsley leaves

Instructions

Add the onion to a larger casserole and cook for 10 minutes. Add peppers, garlic, ginger and spices in it and cook for 3 more minutes. Cover this mixture with wine, and bring it to a boil. Now add tomatoes, bay leaves and saffron and bring it to simmer again. Remove bay leaves and cook for 1 hour and 15 minutes. Add clams and cook for 5 minutes. Add cod, prawn, and lime juice and cook for 15 minutes until fish is completely cooked. Season parsley and serve.

Nutrients: Kcal 177.7, Fat: 5.8g, Total Carbs: 4.7g, Protein: 25.2g

9. Fish With Tomato Sauce

Prep time: 10 minutes

Cook time: 2 hours 10 minutes

Servings: 4

Ingredients

- 1 pound of fish
- 1/3 cup low-sodium broth, vegetable or chicken
- 1 bell pepper, diced
- 1 small onion, diced
- 1 garlic clove, minced
- 15 ounces of diced tomatoes
- 1 tsp of dried herbs
- 1/2 tbsp of Salt
- 1/4 tbsp of pepper

Ingredients

Heat the slow cooker and add onion, bell pepper, broth, tomatoes, and garlic to make a tomato sauce. Add fish on top of it and pour salt, dried herbs and pepper on it. Pour some broth and cook for 2-4 hours on low or 1-2 hours on high.

Nutrients: Kcal 152, Fat: 2.7g, Total Carbs: 8g, Protein: 25.2g

10. Italian Herb Salmon

Prep time: 10 minutes

Cook time: 2 hours

Servings: 4

Ingredients

- 1 pound of salmon
- 1 tbsp of Italian seasonings
- 1 bell pepper, diced
- 15 ounces of diced tomatoes
- 1 tbsp of dried onion flakes
- 1 garlic clove, minced
- 1/2 tsp of salt
- 1/4 tsp of pepper
- 1 tbsp of oil

Instructions

Heat the slow cooker and add diced tomatoes, onion, bell pepper, garlic, Italian seasoning, salt, and pepper. Mix and stir it well. Pour some salt and pepper on salmon and place it in the slow cooker. Cook for 1-2 hours on high or 2-4 hours on low.

Nutrients: Kcal 196, Fat: 5.5g, Total Carbs: 9g, Protein: 26g

11. Salmon With Dill And lemon

Prep time: 10 minutes

Cook time: 2 hours 10 minutes

Servings: 2

Ingredients

- 1 tsp of extra-virgin olive oil
- 1–2 pounds of salmon
- 1 Garlic clove, minced
- 1 lemon, sliced
- Handful fresh dill, loosely chopped
- Salt and pepper to taste

Instructions

Grease the slow cooker with extra-virgin olive oil. Rub the salmon in oil along with garlic, salt, pepper and fresh dill. Place salmon in the slow cooker and cover the top of it with sliced lemons. Cook for 1-2 hours on high or 2-4 hours on low. Serve and enjoy.

Nutrients: Kcal 321, Fat: 12.7g, Total Carbs: 1.8g, Protein: 50.8g

12. Salmon Stew And Coconut Curry

Prep time: 10 minutes

Cook time: 2 hours 5 minutes

Servings: 4

Ingredients

- 1 tbsp of curry powder
- 8 ounces of salmon
- 1/2 cup of water
- 1 bell pepper, diced
- 1/2 small red onion, diced
- 313.5 ounces of light coconut milk
- 1 tsp of finely chopped ginger
- 1 1/2 tsp of salt
- 1/2 tsp of coriander
- 1/4 tsp of pepper

Instructions

Place all the Ingredients in a slow cooker. Give it a good mix and cook for 1-2 hours on low. Serve and enjoy.

Nutrients: Kcal 427, Fat: 18g, Total Carbs: 15g, Protein: 59g

13. Mixed Fish Pie

Prep time: 10 minutes

Cook time: 2 hours

Servings: 6

Ingredients

- 2 ounces of butter
- 2 ounces of plain flour
- 40 fl oz of milk
- 150 fl oz of fish stock
- 1 leek, thinly sliced
- 2.5 ounces of cheddar cheese
- 1 bay leaf
- 1 pound of mixed fish, salmon, smoked haddock, skinned and cubed

Instructions

Grease the saucepan with oil and fry leeks until turned softens. Put it on a plate. Add butter, flour and milk to the saucepan and bring it to a boil while constantly stirring. Pour stock and cheese in it to make a smooth mixture. Add fish to a slow cooker and cover it with sauce. Cook for 2-3 hours on low.

Nutrients: Kcal 455, Fat: 15.7g, Total Carbs: 50.5g, Protein: 27.1g

14. White Fish Gratin

Prep time: 20 minutes

Cook time: 2 hours

Servings: 6

Ingredients

- 3 pounds of frozen, white fish fillet
- 1 cup of Cheddar cheese, shredded
- 6 tbsp of butter
- 3 tbsp of flour
- 1/2 tbsp of dry mustard
- 1/4 tbsp of ground nutmeg
- 1 1/4 cup of milk
- 1 1/2 tsp of lemon juice
- 1 1/2 tsp of salt

Instructions

Grease a saucepan with butter. Add flour, salt, dry mustard, and nutmeg in a saucepan and stir to make them smooth. Add milk while constantly stirring to make it thickened. Place the fish in a slow cooker and cover it completely with cheese sauce over it. Cook for 1-2 hours until fish flaked easily.

Nutrients: Kcal 413, Fat: 21g, Total Carbs: 6g, Protein: 47g

15. Salmon Chowder

Prep time: 5 minutes

Cook time: 3 hours, 10 minutes

Servings: 4

Ingredients

- 1 tbsp of cooking Oil
- 10 oz of Salmon fillet
- 50 ounces of cream
- 2 tbsp of butter
- 1 spicy red chili pepper
- 4 onions
- 3/4 ounces of celery
- 5 ounces of carrot
- 4 potatoes
- 40 fl oz of fish stock
- 1 Bay Leaf
- 1 lime
- Salt and pepper to taste
- 5 ounces of fresh parsley

Instructions

Add oil to a frypan and cook all the vegetables for 10 minutes. Add fish stock, salt and pepper and cook for 2 minutes. Transfer it to a slow cooker, add bay leaf, cook on low for 2.5 hours. Now add butter, cream and lime juice. Cook until butter melts. Add salmon fillet and cook for around 30 minutes until salmon flakes easily.

Nutrients: Kcal 338, Fat: 17g, Total Carbs: 33g, Protein: 15g

16. Fish Chowder With Shrimps

Prep time: 30 minutes

Cook time: 4 hours

Servings: 9

Ingredients

- 1 cup of scallops
- 1 cup of shrimp
- 1/4 pound of halibut, cut into bite-size pieces
- 12 ounces of evaporated milk
- 4 slices of chopped bacon
- 1 onion, chopped
- 2 cloves of garlic, minced
- 10 fl oz of stock
- 1 cup of fresh corn
- 2 large potatoes, diced
- 3 stalks of celery, diced
- 2 large carrots, diced
- ground black pepper to taste
- 1/2 tsp of red pepper flakes

Instructions

Grease the skillet, add bacon and cook for 5-8 minutes until browned. Stir onion and garlic in bacon and cook for 5 minutes, until onion becomes soft. Transfer the mixture to a slow cooker and add stock mixed with corn, potatoes, celery, and carrots. Season with salt, black pepper and red pepper flakes. Cook for 3 hours on high. Add shrimp, halibut and scallops to the slow cooker and cook for more than 1 hour. Put evaporated milk in chowder and serve.

Nutrients: Kcal 190, Fat: 5g, Total Carbs: 20g, Protein: 13g

17. Salmon With Chili And Lime

Prep time: 5 minutes

Cook time: 3 hours 5 minutes

Servings: 1

Ingredients

- 10 ounces of salmon fillet
- 2 cups of fish stock
- 1/3-1/2 cup of cream
- 2 onions
- 3/4 oz of celery
- 1/3 cup of carrot
- 2 potatoes
- 1 bay leaf
- 1 tbsp of cooking oil
- 2 tbsp of butter
- 1 spicy red chili pepper
- 1 lime
- Salt and pepper to taste
- 1 tbsp of fresh parsley

Instructions

Add oil to a frypan. Put onions, carrots, celery and potato in a frypan and cook for 10 minutes. Place the vegetables in a slow cooker and add stock with salt and pepper. Add bay leaf and cook for 2.5 hours. Now add butter, cream, chili and lime juice.

Nutrients: Kcal 269, Fat: 7.5g, Total Carbs: 9.8g, Protein: 38.1g

18. Delicious Seafood Stew

Prep time: 30 minutes

Cook time: 3 hours 30 minutes

Servings: 6

Ingredients

- 28 oz of crushed tomatoes
- 4 cups of vegetable broth
- 1/2 cup of white wine
- 2 cloves garlic, minced
- 1 small onion, diced
- 1 tsp of dried thyme
- 1 tsp of dried basil
- 1 tsp of dried/chopped cilantro
- 1/2 tsp of celery salt
- 1/2 tsp of salt
- 1/2 tsp of pepper
- 1/4 tsp of red pepper flakes
- Pinch of cayenne pepper
- 1 pound of seafood, salmon, rockfish and large shrimp
- 1 pound of baby potatoes, scrubbed and cut

Instructions

Add broth, tomatoes, wine, garlic, onion, thyme, basil, cilantro, celery salt, salt, pepper, red pepper flakes and a pinch of cayenne pepper into the slow cooker and cook for 3 hours on high or 6 hours on low. Now boil potatoes by adding them in a separate saucepan for 15 minutes, until it gets soft. Season the seafood with salt and pepper. Add seafood to the slow cooker and cook for 30 minutes more until seafood is completely cooked.

Nutrients: Kcal 177, Fat: 5.8g, Total Carbs: 4.7g, Protein: 25.2g

19. Fish Risotto

Prep time: 20 minutes

Cook time: 1 hour 5 minutes

Servings: 6

Ingredients

- 1 pound of salmon fillet, skinned and diced
- 3 tbsp of fresh dill, chopped
- 1/2 cup/12.5 oz of white wine
- 75 fl oz of vegetable broth, hot
- 2 tbsp of olive oil
- 4 ounces of shallots, chopped
- 1/2 piece of cucumber
- 1 1/4 cup of arborio rice
- 1 green onion/scallions, chopped
- 1 pinch of salt
- Ground pepper to taste

Instructions

Add the shallot and cucumber in a pan, sauté for 2-3 minutes, with occasional stirring. Cover and cook for 15 minutes on low heat. Add rice grains, then sauté for 1 minute. Transfer in the slow cooker and add hot broth and wine. Cook for 45 minutes more. Add the salmon pieces and season with salt and pepper. Cover and cook for a further 15 min, or until the rice is tender and the salmon is cooked. Stir for 5 minutes in chopped dill and green onion. Serve.

Nutrients: Kcal 320, Fat: 7g, Total Carbs: 41g, Protein: 25g

20. Fish Stew In Coconut Milk

Prep time: 15 minutes

Cook time: 4 hours 15 minutes

Servings: 2

Ingredients

- 1 pound of white fish
- 25 fl oz of coconut milk
- 75 fl oz of tomato sauce
- 1 medium courgette
- 5 large carrots, peeled
- 3 large tomatoes - 1 tsp of garlic puree
- 1 tsp of coriander - 1 tsp of thyme
- 1 tbsp of garlic puree
- 1 small red pepper, diced
- 3 tbsp of coriander - 1 tbsp of paprika
- 1 tsp of rosemary - Salt & pepper to taste

Instructions

Add tomatoes, courgette and carrot to a slow cooker. Add the tomato sauce along with garlic puree, coriander, thyme, salt and pepper. Stir and cook for 2 hours on low. Add whitefish and season with salt, pepper and garlic puree. Cook for a further 1 hour on low. Drain the excess tomato sauce, then add the coconut milk and stir it well. Season with salt, pepper and red pepper. Cook for another 1 hour on low and then serve.

Nutrients: Kcal 335, Fat: 21g, Total Carbs: 13g, Protein: 27g

21. Marinara Cod

Prep time: 10 minutes

Cook time: 2 hours

Servings: 6

Ingredients

- 1.07 pound of cod fillet
- 1 yellow onion, thinly sliced
- 2 cups of diced tomatoes
- 1 sweet, red cubanelle peppers
- 3 garlic cloves minced
- 4 thymes, sprigs
- 1/2 cup of white wine, dry
- 1/2 cup of stock
- 1 cup of white mushroom, sliced
- 1 tbsp of capers
- 1/2 tsp of crushed, black pepper
- 1 tsp of salt

Instructions

Add onions and cubanelle pepper in hot oil in the slow cooker. When onions and peppers are softened, then sauté mushrooms in the oil. Now add tomatoes, thyme sprigs, capers, and wine; bring it to simmer. Add stock, salt and pepper. Put cod in the slow cooker and cover it with sauce on it. Cook on high for 2 hours or on low for 2-4 hours.

Nutrients: Kcal 243, Fat: 8g, Total Carbs: 11g, Protein: 30g

22. Salmon With Lentil Curry

Prep time: 20 minutes

Cook time: 4 hours 15 minutes

Servings: 6

Ingredients

- 2.5 ounces of brown rice
- 40 fl oz of reduced-fat coconut milk
- 8 ounces of Red Lentils
- 3 salmon fillets
- 10 ounces of cherry tomatoes
- 1/2 piece of ginger, finely grated
- 2 tbsp of tomato purée
- 7.5 fl oz of water
- 6 cardamom pods
- 2 cloves garlic, sliced
- 2 red chilies, finely sliced
- Lemon juice
- 2 tbsp of chopped parsley

Instructions

Put rinsed lentils in the slow cooker with coconut milk, tomato purée, garam masala, cardamom, ginger, garlic, chili, tomatoes and 75ml water. Cook on high for 3 hours. Put salmon in the slow cooker and cook for more than 1 hour. Cook brown rice accordingly, in a separate stencil. Mix the lemon juice and parsley into the curry, serve with the rice and lemon wedges.

Nutrients: Kcal 427, Fat: 18g, Total Carbs: 15g, Protein: 59g

23. Fish Stew With Garlic and Pancetta

Prep time: 15 minutes

Cook time: 4 hours

Servings: 4

Ingredients

- 4 ounces of smoked pancetta, diced
- 1/2 pound of swordfish fillets
- 20 fl oz of white wine
- 15 ounces of squid tubes
- 20 ounces of chopped tomatoes
- 4 tbsp of olive oil
- 3 garlic cloves, crushed
- 1 tsp of chili flakes
- 1 grated zest of lemon
- 2 tbsp of finely chopped parsley
- Salt to taste
- Freshly ground black pepper to taste

Instructions

Add oil to a pan and cook pancetta and garlic for 2 minutes. Stir in the chili flakes and chopped tomatoes and cook for about 3 minutes. Transfer it to the slow cooker. Season the swordfish and cook for about 1 minute in a greasy fry pan. Add the fish to the slow cooker. Pour the wine into the hot pan, bring it to simmer, then add to the slow cooker. Now add the squid, cook for 4 hours on high or 8 hours on low. Season with parsley and zest of lemon.

Nutrients: Kcal 231, Fat: 3g, Total Carbs: 10g, Protein: 35g

24. Cod With Red Curry

Prep time: 15 minutes

Cook time: 2 hours

Servings: 4

Ingredients

- 1 pound of codfish fillet
- 215 oz of light coconut milk
- 12 oz of carrots
- 3 tbsp of red curry paste
- 1 tsp of ground ginger
- 1 tbsp of curry powder
- 1 tsp of garlic powder
- 1 red bell pepper, sliced
- 1 green onion
- Salt and pepper to taste

Instructions

Add curry paste, curry powder, ground ginger and garlic powder in coconut milk. Add them to the slow cooker. Now add bell pepper, carrots and cod to the sauce. Cook on low for 2 hours. Season with salt, green onion and pepper before serving.

Nutrients: Kcal 202, Fat: 7.5g, Total Carbs: 9.5g, Protein: 25.3g

25. Monkfish Curry

Prep time: 15 minutes

Cook time: 4 hours

Servings: 4

Ingredients

- 1/2 pound of fresh skinless, monkfish fillet
- 25 fl oz of cold water
- 5 ounces of desiccated coconut
- 8.5 ounces of chopped tomatoes
- 1 red pepper
- 1 green pepper
- 1 medium onion
- 1/2 of fresh root ginger
- 2 garlic cloves
- 1 long green chili
- 1/2 tbsp of fresh coriander
- 1 tbsp of oil
- 2 tbsp of curry paste
- 1 tsp of flaked sea salt
- 1 tsp of caster sugar
- 1 red pepper
- 1 green pepper

Instructions

Add oil to a large frying pan and fry the onion for 3–5 minutes. Add garlic and ginger and cook for a further minute. Stir the curry paste into the pan and fry for a few seconds. Transfer the Ingredients to the slow cooker and stir in chopped tomatoes, coriander, coconut, chili, salt, sugar and water; cover with the lid and cook on high for 3–4 hours or on low for 4–6 hours. Add peppers to the slow cooker. Place the fish on top of the slow cooker, cover it again, and cook for a further hour on high until the fish is tender.

Nutrients: Kcal 433, Fat: 24.5g, Total Carbs: 21.5g, Protein: 31.0g

26. Kerala Fish Coconut Curry

Prep time: 20 minutes

Cook time: 2 hours 30 minutes

Servings: 4

Ingredients

- 12-15 oz of coconut milk
- 3 cloves garlic, minced
- 2 to 3 tbsp of oil
- 10 to 12 Kari leaves
- 1/2 tsp of ground cloves
- 1 tsp of ground cinnamon
- 2 tsp of ground fennel seeds
- 2 tsp of red chili
- 2 tbsp of coriander
- 1 tsp of ground black pepper
- 1 1/2 tsp of salt
- 1/2 cup of water
- 1 tbsp of oil
- 2 medium onions, sliced thin
- 2 or 3 of fresh ginger
- Lemon wedges,
- Juice of 2 lemons
- 1 tsp turmeric - 1/2 tsp salt
- 1 1/2 pound of white fish fillets, red snapper or tilapia

Instructions

Heat the oil in a skillet. Add the onions, chilies, ginger, Kari leaves and fry for 2 minutes until the onions get soft. Transfer to the slow cooker. Add all spices and stir in coconut milk. Cook for 2-4 hours on low. Season fish with lemon juice, turmeric, and salt and marinate for 20 minutes. Fry the marinated fish in oil for 1 to 2 minutes on each side until it gets lightly browned. Place the fish aside. Now transfer all the pieces of fish in curry and bring it to simmer for another minute. Serve hot, garnish with lemon wedges.

Nutrients: Kcal 160, Fat: 15g, Total Carbs: 45g, Protein: 12g

27. Cooked Shrimps With Rice

Prep time: 20 minutes

Cook time: 1 hour

Servings: 8

Ingredients

- 1 pound of large shrimp
- 28 ounces of diced tomatoes
- 1 pound of smoked sausage, sliced
- 1 cup of long-grain white rice
- 1 white onion, diced
- 3 ribs celery, diced
- 1 green bell pepper, diced
- 3 cloves garlic, diced
- 1 tbsp of dried oregano
- 2 bay leaves
- 1 to 2 tbsp of creole seasoning
- 1/2 tsp of salt
- 1/2 tsp of black pepper
- Fresh, chopped, parsley

Instructions

Put sausages, onion, celery, bell pepper, garlic, tomatoes, oregano, bay leaves, and creole seasoning in a slow cooker. Cook on high for 3 hours or on low for 4 to 5 hours. Add shrimp to the slow cooker, cover, and cook on high for more than 30 minutes until the shrimp is well cooked. Cook rice in a separate pan, accordingly. Remove bay leaves from the slow cooker. Season with salt and pepper to taste and garnish with fresh chopped parsley. Stir the cooked rice into the slow cooker and serve.

Nutrients: Kcal 329, Fat: 5.9g, Total Carbs: 20g, Protein: 13g

CHAPTER 5:

Vegetarian Meals

1. Quinoa With Corn Chowder

Prep time: 30 minutes

Cook time: 4 hours

Servings: 4

Ingredients

- 1 tbsp of olive oil
- 1 finely chopped onion
- 2 tsp of garlic, minced
- 1 tsp of ginger, minced
- 2 potatoes medium-sized
- 1/2 tsp of red pepper
- 5 ounces of green beans, chopped
- 1 pound of vegetarian stock
- 4 ounces of quinoa
- 1 tsp of ground coriander
- 1 tbsp of paprika
- 1 tsp of dried or fresh Italian herbs
- 1 bay leaf
- Salt and black pepper to taste
- 17.6 ounces of frozen sweetcorn
- 8.8 ounces of frozen peas
- 3 finely sliced spring onions

Instructions

Take a slow cooker. Add finely chopped onion, garlic and ginger in olive oil, and sauté it. Add potatoes, chopped beans and red pepper and sauté for more than 5 minutes. Add all Ingredients except sweetcorn, peas and spring onion. Cover and cook for 3-4 hours on low flame. Add frozen corn and peas to a slow cooker and cook for another half hour on a high flame. Before serving, stir in spring onions.

Nutrients: Kcal 313, Fat: 9g, Total Carbs: 48g, Protein: 12g

2. Pea Risotto And Green Beans

Prep time: 15 minutes

Cook time: 2 hours 30 minutes

Servings: 4

Ingredients

- 1 tbsp of olive oil
- 4.4 ounces of sliced frozen green beans
- 4.4 ounces of frozen peas
- Parmesan cheese shavings
- 0.06 ounces of butter
- 1 large red onion, chopped
- 2 cloves of garlic, chopped
- 8.8 ounces of risotto rice
- 43 ounces of hot vegetable stock
- salt and pepper to taste
- 2 heaped tsp of green pesto
- 1 handful rocket leaf

Instructions

Take a large, high-sided pan. Add butter and fry onions. Add garlic and rice. Stir and cook for 1 minute. Add salt and pepper in half of the vegetable stock and bring the mixture to a boil. Add the mixture to the slow cooker and cook for 2 hours, on slow. Reheat the remaining vegetable stock with green pesto and add it to the slow cooker and stir. Place all the vegetables on the rice and cook for another 30 minutes on low, with no lid. Garnish with parmesan cheese and rocket leaves before serving.

Nutrients: Kcal 514, Fat: 6g, Total Carbs: 95g, Protein: 17g

3. Slow Cooker Chili Veggie

Prep time: 20 minutes

Cook time: 8 hours

Servings: 6

Ingredients

- 2 thinly sliced courgettes
- 14.1 ounces of drained chickpeas
- 14.1 ounces of whole plum tomatoes
- 1 chopped onion
- 2 sliced carrots
- 2 sliced stalks of celery
- 1 chopped red pepper
- 1 tsp chili powder
- 1 green chili, chopped
- 2 cloves of garlic, minced
- 1 tbsp of dried oregano
- 2 tsp of ground cumin
- 1 tsp of salt

Instructions

Combine all the Ingredients and cover in a slow cooker. Cook on slow for 6-8 hours or on high for 3-4 hours. Garnish with chopped chili and serve.

Nutrients: Kcal 263, Fat: 2.5g, Total Carbs: 51.4g, Protein: 12.9g

4. Cauliflower And Pumpkin Curry

Prep time: 15 minutes

Cook time: 4 hours

Servings: 6

Ingredients

- 1 cauliflower, cut in large chunks
- 1 pumpkin, seeded, peeled and cut
- 13.5 ounces of coconut milk
- 2.1 ounces of Thai red curry paste
- 2 cloves of garlic, minced
- 1 finely minced onion

Instructions

Cook onion and garlic with red curry paste until mixed well on a high flame in the slow cooker. Add pumpkin and cauliflower to a slow cooker. Now add coconut milk gradually to the mixture and cook on slow for 4 hours.

Nutrients: Kcal 227, Fat: 4g, Total Carbs: 35g, Protein: 14g

5. Vegan Chili With Beans

Prep time: 20 minutes

Cook time: 4 hours

Servings: 8

Ingredients

- 8 oz hot water
- 3 tbsp of plain flour
- 12 oz soya minced
- 14 ounces of kidney beans
- 1 large, chopped red onion
- 4 celeries of celery
- 2 chopped red peppers
- 4 bay leaves
- 2 tbsp of chili powder
- 3 tbsp of treacle
- 8 oz of water
- 1 vegetable stock cube
- 1 tsp of hot sauce
- A handful of chopped fresh coriander
- Salt and black pepper to taste

Instructions

Combine minced kidney beans, minced soya, onion, celery, red peppers, bay leaves, chili powder, treacle, stock, coriander, hot sauce, salt, pepper and water in a slow cooker and cook on high for 3 hours. Take hot water and dissolve plain flour in it. Pour the mixture in chili and cook for a further 1 hour.

Nutrients: Kcal 219, Fat: 1.5g, Total Carbs: 38g, Protein: 15g

6. Cheesy Chickpeas

Prep time: 15 minutes

Cook time: 6 hours

Servings: 4

Ingredients

- 12 ounces of rinsed and dried chickpeas
- 1 ounce of parmesan rind
- 3.5 ounces of crumbled feta cheese
- 1 tsp of turmeric - 1 tsp of smoked paprika
- 1 tsp of garam masala
- 1 tsp ground ginger
- 1 tsp of curry powder
- 0.5 tsp of ground black pepper
- 2 tbsp of olive oil - 1 large onion
- 2 minced tomatoes
- 2 cloves of garlic, minced
- 0.5 tsp salt
- 1.5 ounces of parmesan rind
- 1 tsp of tamarind paste
- 10 pitted green olives
- 0.5 ounces of diced butternut squash
- 1 bay leaf - 1 tbsp lemon juice
- 2 tbsp of chopped parsley

Instructions

Take a slow cooker and add turmeric, smoked paprika, garam masala, grounded ginger, curry powder, black pepper in it and cook until fragrant. Add olive oil to the mixture and cook for 10 minutes on high heat to infuse the oil with spices. Add the onions and cook for 1 hour until the mixture becomes soft. Now add tomatoes, garlic, dried chickpeas, salt, parmesan rind, tamarind paste, green olives, butternut squash and the bay leaf and cook on high heat for 4 hours or on low for 6 hours. Put lemon juice, black pepper, chopped parsley and feta cheese, mix it well and stir. Garnish some parsley or fresh yogurt before serving.

Nutrients: Kcal 110, Fat: 9g, Total Carbs: 0g, Protein: 7g

7. Potato And Leek Soup

Prep time: 20 minutes

Cook time: 6 hours

Servings: 8

Ingredients

- 3 large sliced leeks
- 1 pound of potatoes
- 20 ounces of vegetable stock
- 5 ounces of double or single cream
- Salt and pepper, to taste
- Oil for cooking

Instructions

Chop the potatoes, add them to the frying pan with leeks and some oil, and cook until it turns brown. Take the mixture of potatoes and leek in a slow cooker. Add vegetable stock, salt and pepper to it and cover with a lid. Cook for 6 hours, on a slow heat. Add cream to the mixture to make a smooth consistency and serve hot.

Nutrients: Kcal 310, Fat: 15g, Total Carbs: 34g, Protein: 9g

8. Quorn Chili Veggie Bowl

Prep time: 15 minutes

Cook time: 8 hours

Servings: 8

Ingredients

- 14 ounces of corn
- 21 ounces of passata
- 14 ounces of rinsed and drained kidney beans
- 1.8 oz of water
- 1 diced onion
- 2 sticks celery, diced
- 1 diced green pepper
- 2 cloves of minced garlic
- 1/2 tbsp of chili powder
- 1 tsp of salt
- 1 tsp of ground cumin
- 1 tsp of ground coriander
- 3/4 tsp of dried oregano
- 1/4 tsp of ground black pepper

Instructions

Take a slow cooker and add all the Ingredients to it. Cover it with a lid and cook for 8 hours on low. Serve and enjoy.

Nutrients: Kcal 198.4, Fat: 6.4g, Total Carbs: 23.6g, Protein: 13.4g

9. Chili And Bean Combo

Prep time: 15 minutes

Cook time: 3 hours

Servings: 4

Ingredients

- 1 red onion
- 14 ounces of black beans
- 14 ounces of pinto beans
- 14 ounces of cannellini beans
- 14 ounces of chopped tomatoes
- 3-4 medium garlic clove
- 3 tsp of chili powder
- 1 tsp of salt
- 1 tsp of black pepper

Instructions

Rinse and drain all the beans before putting them in a slow cooker. Add tomatoes to a slow cooker along with all the beans, chopped onions, garlic, chili powder, pepper and salt. Cook for around 3 hours on low heat, if desired, then cook for 1 hour further.

Nutrients: Kcal 264, Fat: 9.6g, Total Carbs: 34g, Protein: 16g

10. Easy Vegetable Soup

Prep time: 20 minutes

Cook time: 8 hours

Servings: 4

Ingredients

- 50 ounces of water
- 2 cubes of stock
- 5 ounces of rinsed lentils
- 2-3 chopped carrots
- 2 chopped potatoes
- 1/2 chopped turnip
- 1 chopped onion
- Salt and pepper to taste

Instructions

Add water to a slow cooker and put cubes of stock in it. Stir to dissolve the cubes of stock completely. Add all the vegetables along with turnip, potatoes and carrots. Stir it well and cook for 8 hours until all the vegetables become tender. If desired, then stir some liquidizer in it to make a smooth puree.

Nutrients: Kcal 159, Fat: 3.8g, Total Carbs: 26g, Protein:5.8g

11. Salty Baked Potatoes

Prep time: 10 minutes

Cook time: 4 hours,30 minutes

Servings: 4

Ingredients

- 1 tbsp of olive oil
- 4 potatoes
- 4 pieces of aluminum foil
- Salt to taste

Instructions

Take potatoes in a dish and scrub it with a fork. Rub the potatoes in extra virgin olive oil and add some salt to taste. Wrap the potatoes in aluminum foil and put them in a slow cooker. Cook the potatoes on a high for 4 hours or low for 6 hours until tender.

Nutrients: Kcal 161, Fat: 0.2g, Total Carbs: 37g, Protein: 4.3g

12. Aubergine, Mushroom And Potato Curry

Prep time: 20 minutes

Cook time: 6 hours

Servings: 4

Ingredients

- 15 ounces of chopped mushrooms
- 1 medium, diced aubergine
- 4 medium, diced potatoes
- 30 ounces of vegetable stock
- 1 tbsp of flour
- 1 tbsp of tomato puree or ketchup
- 4 tbsp of cooking oil
- 2-4 tbsp of curry paste
- 1 piece of fresh, grated ginger
- 2 cloves of garlic crushed
- 1 green chili finely chopped
- 4 finely sliced onions

Instructions

Add onions, aubergine, potatoes and mushrooms to a large pan and cook for 2 minutes. Now add flour, green chili, garlic, ginger, curry paste and tomato puree in a pan and cook for 1 minute. Add vegetable stock to a pan, stir everything together, cook for more than 5 minutes, and bring it to a boil. Put the curry mixture in a slow cooker and cook for 8 hours on low or 6 hours on high. Serve with rice and freshly chopped coriander.

Nutrients: Kcal 200, Fat: 14g, Total Carbs: 18g, Protein: 2.8g

13. Red Lentil And Pumpkin Soup

Prep time: 15 minutes

Cook time: 8 hours

Servings: 8

Ingredients

- 1 leek
- 10 ounces of dried red lentil
- 52 ounces of pumpkin
- 40 ounces of vegetable stock
- 2 tbsp of curry

Instructions

Add chopped leek and pumpkin in a slow cooker. Pour dried red lentil on top of the pumpkin and stir. Now add curry in vegetable stock and pour it in the slow cooker, over vegetables. Mix all the vegetables. Cook for 6-8 hours on low or 4 hours on high. When the curry is ready, mash all the vegetables with a potato masher, if desired.

Nutrients: Kcal 241, Fat: 11g, Total Carbs: 27g, Protein: 9.5g

14. Beans And Barley Curry

Prep time: 20 minutes

Cook time: 8 hours

Servings: 2

Ingredients

- 4 tbsp of pearl barley
- 14 ounces of red kidney beans
- 14 ounces of chopped tomatoes
- 18 ounces of vegetable stock
- 1 chopped onion
- 1 chopped celery stick
- 3 garlic cloves, minced
- 1tbsp of olive oil
- 1 tbsp of mushroom ketchup
- 1 bay leaf
- Salt and pepper to taste

Instructions

Add onion, chopped celery stick and garlic in a saucepan and cook in oil until it gets soft. Add this mixture to a slow cooker, and put all the remaining Ingredients in it. Cook on low for 6 hours and serve.

Nutrients: Kcal 110, Fat: 1g, Total Carbs: 22g, Protein: 4g

15. Chia And Blueberry Quinoa Bowl

Prep time: 5 minutes

Cook time: 6 hours

Servings: 6

Ingredients

- 12 ounces of quinoa
- 10 ounces of blueberries
- 2 ounces of chia seeds
- 2 ounces of honey
- 33 ounces of water
- 33 ounces of soya milk

Instructions

Add quinoa, blueberries, chia seeds, soy milk, honey and water to the slow cooker. Cook on low for 6-8 hours.

Nutrients: Kcal 381, Fat: 6.4g, Total Carbs: 69.1g, Protein: 13.7g

16. Creamy Leek Soup

Prep time: 20 minutes

Cook time: 5 hours

Servings: 4

Ingredients

- 7 fl oz of single cream
- 20 fl oz of vegetable stock
- 3 potatoes, diced
- 2 tbsp of olive oil
- 4 large sliced leeks
- 1 clove of garlic, minced
- Salt and pepper to taste
- Parsley to garnish

Instructions

Add leeks, potatoes and garlic in a pan, cook until they get brown. Now add this to a slow cooker and put the remaining seasonings in it. Cook for 4-5 hours on low. Add liquidizer to puree the soup, and add cream. Garnish with parsley and serve.

Nutrients: Kcal 50, Fat: 2.2g, Total Carbs: 6.4g, Protein: 1.5g

17. Easy Forest Risotto

Prep time: 25 minutes

Cook time: 2 hours

Servings: 4

Ingredients

- 21 ounces of wild mushrooms, chopped
- 14 ounces of Carnaroli rice
- 20 oz of vegetable stock
- 2 cloves of minced garlic
- 1 chopped onion
- 3 ounces of salted butter
- 10 ounces of fresh nasturtium seeds
- Salt and pepper, to taste
- 2 ounces of grated Parmesan cheese

Instructions

Fry the onions in butter. Add garlic in it, cook for 3-4 minutes. Add mushrooms and cook for 5-6 minutes, until they turn golden brown. Add the rice to the pan and stir well to coat with butter. Add vegetable stock and bring it to boil. Transfer the mixture to the slow cooker and cook for 2 hours. In the last 30 minutes, add nasturtium seeds. Stir and add parmesan cheese before serving.

Nutrients: Kcal 210, Fat: 3g, Total Carbs: 37g, Protein: 6g

18. Cheesy Sweet Corns

Prep time: 20 minutes

Cook time: 4 hours

Servings: 8

Ingredients

- 8 ounces of grated Cheddar cheese
- 11 ounces of cubed cream cheese
- 18 ounces of frozen sweetcorn
- 4 tbsp of butter
- 3 tbsp of water
- 3 tbsp of milk
- 2 tbsp of sugar

Instructions

Add sweet corn, butter, milk, sugar, and water to a slow cooker. Mix all the Ingredients, and cook for 3-4 hours on low. Add cream cheese and cheddar cheese to it. Cook well until cheese melts. Stir well before serving.

Nutrients: Kcal 99, Fat: 1.5g, Total Carbs: 19g, Protein: 3g

19. Tomato Soup

Prep time: 10 minutes

Cook time: 1 hour

Servings: 4

Ingredients

- 4 tins of chopped tomatoes
- 25 oz of vegetable stock
- 4 large chopped carrots
- 4 onions, chopped
- 4 cloves of chopped garlic
- 2 chopped celery sticks
- 2 small potatoes, diced
- Olive oil
- 1 handful fresh rosemary
- 1 handful fresh parsley
- Dried or fresh chili peppers
- Salt and pepper to taste

Instructions

Add carrots, onions, garlic, and celery in olive oil and sauté for 4-5 minutes. Add potatoes and cook for 10 minutes. Stir it well. Add dried herbs, chili pepper, tomatoes and salt and cook for 20 minutes. Add stock in the slow cooker and cook for further 40 minutes. When all veggies become soft, blend the mixture in a blender, add stock to consistency, and re-heat.

Nutrients: Kcal 170, Fat: 1.1g, Total Carbs: 36g, Protein: 3.5g

20. Creamy Potatoes

Prep time: 15 minutes

Cook time: 7 hours

Servings: 4

Ingredients

- 1 tin of condensed milk of mushroom soup
- 8 sliced potatoes
- 4 slices of pancetta, chopped
- 10 ounces of grated Parmesan cheese
- Salt and pepper to taste

Instructions

Add butter to a slow cooker to grease it well. Add all the Ingredients to a slow cooker and cook on low for 7-9 hours. If desired, more seasoning can be added before serving.

Nutrients: Kcal 261, Fat: 17g, Total Carbs: 21g, Protein: 7.6g

21. Carrot Glaze

Prep time: 10 minutes

Cook time: 7 hours

Servings: 4

Ingredients

- 18 ounces of carrots
- 2 ounces of butter
- 6 tbsp of orange marmalade
- 1 tbsp of water
- Salt and pepper to taste

Instructions

Add all the Ingredients to a slow cooker. Cover the slow cooker with a lid and cook for 7-9 hours, until carrots become soft and tender.

Nutrients: Kcal 160, Fat: 7.6g, Total Carbs: 22g, Protein: 1.4g

22. Slow Cooker Cassoulet

Prep time: 20 minutes

Cook time: 9 hours

Servings: 8

Ingredients

- 16 ounces of dry haricot beans, soaked
- 10 oz of mushroom stock
- 2 tbsp of olive oil
- 1 onion
- 2 carrots, peeled and diced
- 1 vegetable stock cube
- 1 bay leaf
- 4 sprigs of fresh parsley
- 1 sprig of fresh rosemary
- 1 sprig fresh lemon thyme, chopped
- 1 sprig of fresh savory
- 1 large potato, cubed

Instructions

Add oil in a pan and cook carrots and onions in it until they soften. Combine beans, carrots and onion, mushroom stock, vegetable stock cube and bay leaf in a slow cooker and cover with water. Tie parsley, rosemary, thyme and savory together in a knot, and add to the cooker. Cook on Low for 8 hours. Add potatoes, and cook further for 1 hour. Remove herbs before serving.

Nutrients: Kcal 774, Fat: 47g, Total Carbs: 43g, Protein: 39g

23. Delicious Spaghetti Squash

Prep time: 5 minutes

Cook time: 4 hours

Servings: 4

Ingredients

- 30 oz of water
- 1 whole spaghetti squash

Instructions

Add squash in a slow cooker for 10-15 minutes. Now add water to it and cook for 4 to 6 hours on low. Place squash on a cutting board and let it cool. Remove all the seeds from it and make strands like spaghetti with the help of a fork. Serve and Enjoy.

Nutrients: Kcal 259, Fat: 2.5g, Total Carbs: 62g, Protein: 6.3g

24. Slow Cooker Vegan Soup

Prep time: 20 minutes

Cook time: 3 hour

Servings: 4

Ingredients

- 1 dessert spoon vegan stock powder
- 5 ounces of fine green beans
- 5 ounces of sugar snap peas
- 49 ounces of chopped tomatoes
- 20 ounces of red kidney beans
- 1 thinly sliced carrot
- 1 thinly sliced potato
- 4 fresh tomatoes, chopped
- 1 chopped pepper
- 1 tsp of marmite
- Salt and pepper to taste

Instructions

Add vegetables and potatoes to a slow cooker and cover it by adding water. Bring it to boil. Add marmite and vegetable stock powder. Cook for 3 hours on low. Serve and Enjoy.

Nutrients: Kcal 65, Fat: 2.4g, Total Carbs: 7.3g, Protein: 3.4g

25. Cheese Risotto Primavera

Prep time: 20 minutes

Cook time: 2 hours

Servings: 4

Ingredients

- 5 ounces of butter
- 2 tbsp of olive oil
- 8 medium shallots, sliced
- 2 cloves of garlic, minced
- 15 ounces of arborio rice
- 8 oz of white wine
- 30 oz of warmed vegetable stock
- 8 ounces of shelled broad beans
- 15 ounces of asparagus spears, chopped
- 1 courgette, chopped
- 4 ounces of shelled peas
- 4 ounces of grated Parmesan cheese
- 1 large handful of rocket leaves
- Salt and pepper to taste

Instructions

Add half of the butter to a pan and saute shallots and garlic in it. Cook well for 3-4 minutes. Transfer them to a slow cooker. Now add the remaining butter to the same pan and add rice to it. Cover the rice with wine and bring it to simmer for 4-5 minutes, until water is absorbed. Convert it to the slow cooker. Add vegetable stock and other vegetables. Cover with a lid and cook for 2 hours on low. Add parmesan cheese, and rocket leaves in it and stir. If desired, then season again.

Nutrients: Kcal 260, Fat: 7.4g, Total Carbs: 40g, Protein: 11g

CHAPTER 6:

Gluten-Free Recipes

1. Chicken Gravy

Prep time: 25 minutes

Cook time: 9 hours

Servings: 7

Ingredients

- 2 pounds of chicken thigh
- 1 sliced onion
- 1 tbsp of crushed garlic
- 1 tbsp of Worcestershire sauce
- 1 tsp of thyme
- 1/3 cup of cream
- 1/2 cup of dry white wine
- 2 cups of chicken stock Thickener
- 6 tbsp of water
- 6 tbsp of cornstarch

Instructions

Add all the Ingredients to a slow cooker except the water, cream, and cornstarch. On a low flame, let it cook for 7-8 hours. Shred the chicken and added it to the slow cooker. Mix water and cornstarch until it is smooth in a separate bowl. Add the cornstarch mixture and cream to the chicken gravy and stir it. Let the mixture be cooked on high flame for half an hour until it's thickened and hot. Sprinkle it with salt and pepper for seasoning. Serve it in a dish and enjoy while it's hot.

Nutrients: Kcal 400, Fat: 35.7g, Total Carbs: 12g, Protein: 32g

2. Tomato Soup

Prep time: 20 minutes

Cook time: 9 hours

Servings: 7

Ingredients

- 3 diced onions
- 3 diced celeries
- 4 tsp of crushed garlic
- 2 chopped red bell pepper
- 1/2 tsp of sugar
- 3 tbsp pf tomato paste
- 3 tsp of dried oregano
- 3 bay leaves
- 3 tsp of dried basil
- 2 pounds. crushed tomatoes
- 2 cups of chicken stock
- 1 cup of heavy cream

Instructions

Except for the heavy cream, add all the ingredients into the slow cooker. Cook for 7 hours on low. Remove the bay leaves. Mix the Ingredients until smooth. Now add the cream. Season to taste. Now cook for 20 minutes on high or until they are hot. Serve and enjoy your meal.

Nutrients: Kcal: 320, Fat: 13g, Total Carbs: 19g, Protein: 35g

3. Onion Gravy With Sausage

Prep time: 35 minutes

Cook time: 7 hours

Servings: 7

Ingredients

- 3 pounds. of beef sausages (gluten-free)
- 3 cups of beef stock
- 2 tsp of crushed garlic
- 3 tsp of Worcestershire sauce (gluten-free)
- 3 sliced onions
- 4 tbsp of cornstarch (gluten-free)
- 5 tbsp of water

Instructions

Heat the sausage on the frying pan until brown. Add all the Ingredients except for thickeners in the slow cooker. Cook for 7 hours on low. Remove sausages. Mix cornstarch and water and pour into the slow cooker, stir, and season for taste. Add sausages back into the slow cooker and cook for at least 25 minutes. When thickened, serve and enjoy

Nutrients: Kcal: 590, Fat: 47g, Total Carbs: 7g, Protein: 40g

4. Creamy Potato Sausage

Prep time: 20 minutes

Cook time: 9 hours

Servings: 5

Ingredients

- 2 pounds of sliced sausages (gluten-free)
- 2 pounds of chunked potatoes
- 3 tsp of crushed garlic
- 2 cups of heavy cream
- 4 tbsp of Worcestershire sauce
- 2 cups of chicken stock
- 2 sliced onions
- 3 tsp of chopped parsley
- 4 tbsp of cornstarch (gluten-free)
- 5 tbsp of water

Instructions

Add all the Ingredients into the slow cooker, except for thickeners and heavy cream. Cook on low for 8 hours until the potatoes are cooked. Mix cornstarch with water and pour into the slow cooker and stir along with heavy cream. Cook for 30 minutes until thick. Season it and enjoy

Nutrients: Kcal: 500, Fat: 37.4g, Total Carbs: 30g, Protein: 15g, Sodium: 900mg

5. Roasted Lamb

Prep time: 30 minutes

Cook time: 9 hours

Servings: 9

Ingredients

For Roasted Lamb

- 5 pounds of lamb
- 2 tsp of salt
- 1 tsp of pepper
- 2 tsp of garlic
- 2 tbsp of oregano
- 3 tsp of rosemary leaves
- 1 cup of chicken stock

Vegetables

- 2 chopped onions
- 5 chopped carrots
- 2 tsp crushed garlic
- 3 chopped onions

Instructions

Rub garlic, salt, and pepper on the lamb. Heat the oil in a frying pan. Add lamb and brown it from all sides. Transfer it into the slow cooker. Add left Ingredients into the slow cooker. Sprinkle the oregano and rosemary leaves over the meat and vegetables. In the end, add chicken stock. Cook on low for 9 hours. Serve it, and enjoy!

Nutrients: Kcal: 564, Fat: 27g, Total Carbs: 40g, Protein: 40g

6. Sweet Potatoes Soup

Prep time: 20 minutes

Cook time: 7 hours

Servings: 7

Ingredients

- 4 pounds of cubed and peeled sweet potatoes
- 2 chopped carrots
- 2 tsp of grounded cumin
- 2 chopped onions
- 3 tsp of crushed garlic
- 3 stalked and chopped celery
- 25 fl oz of chicken stock
- 8 fl oz of coconut cream

Instructions

Add all the Ingredients except for cream into the slow cooker. Cook until the sweet potatoes are tenders for about 7 hours. Blend the soup until smooth using a blender. Add coconut cream and stir. Cook for more than 30 minutes until hot. Now serve and enjoy!

Nutrients: Kcal: 430, Fat: 16g, Total Carbs: 63g, Protein: 9g

7. Cheesy Chicken Broccoli Rice

Prep time: 10 minutes.

Cook time: 4hours.

Servings: 8

Ingredients

- 1 tbsp of olive oil
- 1 1/2 pounds chicken breasts, cut into chunks
- 1 chopped onion
- 1 coarsely chopped garlic clove
- 1 cup of uncooked grain rice
- 32 oz. of chicken broth
- 1 1/4 tsp of salt
- 1/3 tsp of pepper
- 2 cups of broccoli, chopped
- 1 1/4 cup of dairy-free cheddar cheese

Instructions

Add olive oil, garlic, and chopped onions to the slow cooker. Add the chicken breast pieces, salt, pepper, and rice. Pour broth on top. Mix. Put the lid on of the slow cooker and turn it on high. Cook for 4hours on high. 2 hours later, check to ensure there is still enough liquid inside. If not, add some more warmed-up broth. Half an hour before it's done, add the chopped broccoli and stir. Add more warm broth if needed. Cook for another half an hour until broccoli is bright green and tender. Add the cheese and stir until melted. Season with more salt and pepper if desired. Serve and enjoy

Nutrients: kcal: 271, Fat: 8g, Total Carbs: 26g, Protein: 21g

8. Bangers and Mash

Prep time: 20 minutes

Cook time: 3 hours

Servings: 6

Ingredients

- 16 ounces of sausages, uncooked
- 1 onion, sliced
- Mashed cauliflower

For Gravy

- 2 cups of low sodium beef broth
- 1 tsp of dried thyme
- 1/2 tsp of garlic powder
- 1 tsp of salt or as desired

Instructions

In a slow cooker, Add sausages and onion. In a small bowl, mix gravy Ingredients. Pour gravy into the slow cooker. Stir gently. Cook on high heat for 3 hours. In a small bowl, mix slurry. Pour slurry into the slow cooker and stir. Cook until gravy has thickened to your liking.

Nutrients: Kcal: 365, Fat: 31g, Total Carbs: 6g, Protein: 15g

9. Shepherd's Pie

Prep time: 20 minutes

Cook time: 7 hours

Servings: 6

Ingredients

- 1 pound. of ground beef
- 1 pound. of ground lamb
- 1 medium chopped onion
- 2 tsp of minced garlic
- 12 oz. of frozen peas and carrots
- 14 oz. of diced tomatoes drained
- 3 tbsp of tapioca
- 2 tsp of dried oregano
- 1 tsp of salt
- 1/2 tsp of black pepper
- 48 oz. of mashed potatoes

Instructions

Brown meat in a large skillet over medium-high heat for 6-8 minutes, stirring to break up meat. Add meat to the slow cooker. Add onions and then garlic to the pan and cook until they are tender. Add it to the slow cooker. Add peas, tomatoes, carrots, salt, tapioca, oregano and pepper into the cooker and mix. Cook on low for around 8 hours. Serve and enjoy.

Nutrients: Kcal: 678, Fat: 33g, Total Carbs: 63g, Protein: 35g

10. Beef Stew

Prep time: 20 minutes

Cook time: 7 hours

Servings: 8

Ingredients

- 2 pounds. of beef chunks
- 1/4 tbsp of salt
- 1/4 tbsp of grounded black pepper
- 1 tbsp of olive oil
- 1 diced large white onion
- 2 stalk celeries, cut into pieces
- 1 pound. of potatoes cut into cubes
- 3 large carrots cut into pieces
- 32 oz. of beef broth (gluten-free)
- 1 tbsp of salt
- 1 tbsp of grounded black pepper
- 3 tbsp of tomato puree
- 1 tbsp of Worcestershire sauce (gluten-free)
- 2 minced garlic cloves
- 2 dried bay leaves
- 1 tbsp of dried thyme
- 2 tbsp of cornstarch
- 1 cup of frozen peas

Instructions

Sprinkle salt and pepper on the cubed slices of beef from all sides. Preheat the skillet to medium-high and add olive oil to the skillet. Work in the form of batches and brown the cubed beef on the skillet. Add all the browned beef into the slow cooker. Add all the Ingredients into the slow cooker. Cook beef stew on low heat for 7 hours. When beef is tender, shred the beef with a fork. Remove the bay leaves and discard. Take out a half cup of broth from the slow cooker and mix it in cornstarch. Whisk it until no clumps remain. Now pour the above mixture into the slow cooker and combine with the slow cooker Ingredients. Let it cook for more than 30 minutes. Serve with the fresh chopped parsley.

Nutrients: Kcal: 252.2, fat: 6.6g, Total Carbs: 27.7g, protein: 20.4g

11. Cuban Beef

Prep time: 10 minutes

Cook time: 7 hours

Servings: 5

Ingredients

- 1.1 pounds of stewing steak
- 0.8 pounds of chopped tomatoes
- 2 red peppers, sliced into strips
- 2 sliced onions
- 2 tbsp tomato puree
- 5 crushed garlic cloves
- 1 tsp ground cumin
- 1/2 tsp of turmeric
- 1 tsp of oregano
- 3 bay leaves
- 14 oz. of beef stock
- 1 white or red wine
- 1 tbsp of fresh coriander
- 1 tbsp of white wine vinegar
- Salt and pepper for seasoning

Instructions

Season the meat with salt and pepper, then brown the meat on a frying pan. Add all Ingredients into the slow cooker. Add the meat also. Use slow cooker on high and cook for about 7 hours. Strip the meat inside the slow cooker. Wait for the sauce to be thick. Serve while hot!

Nutrients: Kcal: 280, Fats: 5.8 g, Total Carbs: 17 g, Protein: 35 g

12. Bolognese

Prep time: 15 minutes

Cook time: 8 hours

Servings: 4

Ingredients

- 0.9 pounds of mince
- 1.1 pounds of passata
- 1 tbsp of garlic puree
- 1 tbsp of Italian herbs
- 2 tbsp of tomato puree
- Salt and pepper for seasoning

Instructions

Add all the Ingredients into the slow cooker and mix well. Cook on low for 8 hours. Serve with pasta or rice or anything you fancy!

Nutrients: kcal: 237, Fat: 16g, Total Carbs: 9g, Protein: 15g

13. Apple, Sausage and Bean Casserole

Prep time: 15 minutes

Cook time: 3 1/2 hours

Servings: 6 to 8

Ingredients

- 12 gluten-free sausages
- 1 chopped white and red onion
- 10 chopped slices of bacon
- 3 crushed garlic cloves
- 1 apple that is peeled and sliced into eighth
- 0.3pounds. of chestnut button mushrooms
- 2 tbsp brown sugar
- 3 tbsp of tomato puree
- 6.3 oz. of apple cider
- Herbs
- 2 of 400 g of chopped tomatoes
- 0.8pounds of kidney beans
- 0.8pounds of cannellini beans
- 0.8pounds of butter beans
- 5.2 oz. of vegetable stock (gluten-free)

Instructions

Brown the bacon on a frying pan. Add onions into the frying pan for 10 minutes. Now add chili, garlic, mushrooms, and apple and cook furthermore for about 3 minutes. Now, add all the left Ingredients, keeping in mind to add the stock at the end. Now Pour the recipe into the slow cooker and cook on high for 3 hours. Serve and enjoy

Nutrients: kcal: 314, Fat: 9g, Total Carbs: 34g, Protein: 30g

14. Apple Butter

Prep time: 10 minutes

Cook time: 5 hours

Servings: 5

Ingredients

- 10 apples, chopped
- 2 tbsp of cinnamon
- 3 tbsp of maple syrup, honey, or caster sugar

Instructions

Add all the Ingredients into the slow cooker along with water and cook for about 3 hours. Turn it off and let it cool. Blend until smooth. Turn the heat back on for 2 more hours on low heat till thick. Serve and enjoy!

Nutrients: Kcal: 22, Fat: 0.1g, Total Carbs: 4g, Protein: 0.1g

15. Chili Con Carne

Prep time: 30 minutes

Cook time: 8 hours

Servings: 8

Ingredients

- 1 pound of minced beef
- 1 celery, finely chopped
- 1 chopped onion
- 1 thickly sliced red pepper
- 2 grated garlic cloves
- 2 tbsp of grounded cumin
- 1 tsp of paprika
- 2 tsp of oregano, dried
- 3 tbsp of chipotle chili paste
- 3 tbsp of tomato puree
- 0.8pounds of chopped tomatoes
- 14 oz. of beef stock
- 0.8pounds of black beans
- 5 small dark choco squares

Instructions

Fry the minced beef in a pan for 20 minutes or brown and add to the slow cooker. Add celery, onion, garlic, cumin, pepper, and paprika in the same oil and mix well. Then add into slow cooker. Now add all the remaining Ingredients into the slow cooker except for the beans and choco and cook for 8 hours. Stir in the chocolate and beans for the last 30 minutes of the cooking. Serve and enjoy

Nutrients: Kcal: 280, Fat: 14g, Total Carbs: 18g, Protein: 20g

16. Chicken Casserole

Prep time: 10 minutes

Cook time: 7 hours 15minutes

Servings: 4

Ingredients

- 1/2 tbsp of rapeseed
- 1 finely chopped onion
- 1 1/2 tbsp of flour
- 1 pound of boneless thigh fillets chicken
- 3 crushed garlic cloves
- 0.8 pounds potatoes, halved
- 3 sliced celeries
- 3 diced carrots
- 0.5 pounds of quartered mushrooms
- 0.5 pounds of dried porcini mushrooms
- 44 oz. chicken stock
- 3 tsp of mustard
- 3 bay leaves

Instructions

Fry onions in a frying pan until soft. Put flour, salt, and pepper in a bowl and toss the chicken in it. Now add the chicken and garlic into the pan and cook until it goes brown. Transfer everything into the slow cooker along with the other left Ingredients. Give it a good stir and cook on low for 7 hours. Serve with mustard topping.

Nutrients: Kcal: 388, Fat: 10g, Total Carbs: 31g, Protein: 42g

17. Sweet Potato Turkey Stew

Prep time: 15 minutes

Cook time: 8 hours

Servings: 5

Ingredients

- 5 turkey breasts
- 3 sweet potatoes and normal potatoes
- 3 carrots
- 1 cup of blended tomatoes
- 1 cup of water
- 4 tbsp of paprika
- 3 tbsp of turmeric
- 2 small chopped gingers
- 2 tbsp of cinnamon
- black pepper for sprinkling
- 3 garlic cloves

Instructions

Slice turkey into chunks and ass then into slow cooker. Add tomatoes. Chop and peel a potato, carrots, and sweet potato into small chunks. Add water slowly, garlic and ginger. Add to mix with all other spices. Mix the mixture with a spoon. Serve after 8 hours of cooking.

Nutrients: kcal: 186, Fat: 4.7g, Total Carbs: 2102g, Protein: 1505g

18. Gluten-Free Sausages and Potatoes Stew

Prep time: 15 minutes

Cook time: 8 hours

Servings: 5

Ingredients

- 10 chicken sausages
- 2 sweet potatoes and normal potatoes
- 1 courgette
- 2 tbsp of vegetable stock
- 1 cup of chopped tomatoes
- 1 tsp of cinnamon
- 1 tsp of turmeric
- 2 garlic cloves
- 1 ginger
- 1 tsp of paprika

Instructions

Brown the chicken sausages in the frying pan for 7 minutes or until brown. In the slow cooker, add chopped tomatoes, mixed vegetable stock, chicken, sausages, Peeled and sliced sweet potato and potato and courgette cooked, peel and slice. Mix them all. Now add finely chopped gingers and garlic into the slow cooker. Sprinkle the slices as described in the ingredients. Mix well to ensure vegetables, sausages, and everything is completed soaked and covered in liquid as much as possible. Cook in the slow cooker for 8 hours and serve it hot.

Nutrients: kcal: 540, Fat: 18g, Total Carbs: 34g, Protein: 30g

19. Sweet Potato, Spinach and Peas Curry

Prep time: 15 minutes

Cook time: 4 hours

Servings: 3

Ingredients

- 1 chopped tomato
- 1 onion
- 8.8 oz of sweet potato
- 5.2 oz of chickpeas
- 1/2 tbsp of cumin of turmeric
- 1 tsp of ground coriander
- 1/2 tsp of red chili powder
- 2 tsp of small fresh ginger
- 1 tsp of small crushed garlic
- 5.2 fl. oz. of coconut milk
- 3.5 fl. oz. of vegetable stock
- 2 tsp of corn flour
- 2 oz. of spinach

Instructions

Add all the Ingredients into the slow cooker. Turn it on high for 3 hours until the sweet potato is nice and soft. Corn flour is mixed in water and stirred into the curry, turn the slow cooker on high for a further half an hour to get it thick. Add spinach and serve

Nutrients: Kcal: 365, Fat: 31g, Total Carbs: 6g, Protein: 15g

20. Lentil and Sausages Stew

Prep time: 15 minutes

Cook time: 4 hours

Servings: 5

Ingredients

- 1 can of red lentils
- 8 sausages
- 2 carrots
- 1/2 celeriac
- 1 onion
- 0.8pounds can of tomatoes
- 14 fl. Oz. of beef stock

Instructions

Add the sausages to the slow cooker, and then add the lentils on top of it. Now add in all the ingredients and mix well. Cook on high for 4 hours and serve hot

Nutrients: Kcal: 231, Fat: 4g, Total Carbs: 34g, Protein: 19g

21. Turkish Hash

Prep time: 20 minutes

Cook time: 6 hours.

Servings: 4

Ingredients

- 4 potatoes
- 2 butternut squashes
- 3 carrots
- 2 onions
- 1.5 pounds. of minced turkey
- 15 fl. Oz. of chicken stock
- 1 tbsp of gluten-free Worcestershire sauce
- 2 bay leaves
- 1 tsp of thyme
- 1/2 tsp of sage
- Corn flour and water

Instructions

Place all the vegetables into a slow cooker. Put the minced turkey in a frying pan and cool or fry until brown. Now add turkey into the slow cooker. Now add all the left Ingredients except for. Corn flour and water into the slow cooker and cook on low for about 6 hours. About 5 hours, mix corn flour with a little water and stir to thicken. Leave for the final hour. Serve it hot.

Nutrients: Kcal: 457, Fat: 8g, Total Carbs: 54g, Protein: 40g

22. Meatballs

Prep time: 15 minutes

Cook time: 4 hours

Servings: 12

Ingredients

- 1 cup of gluten-free bread crumbs
- 4 fluid ounces of red wine
- 1 pound ground pork & ground beef
- 1 beaten egg - 1 tbsp of dried oregano
- 2 tsp of dried basil - 1/2 tsp of garlic powder
- 1/2 tsp of onion powder - 1/4 tsp of salt
- 1/8 tsp of ground black pepper
- 2 ounces Parmigiano-
- Reggiano cheese finely grated

For Tomato Sauce

- 28 ounces of can tomato puree
- 3 ounces of tomato paste
- 1 tbsp of dried oregano
- 2 tsp of dried basil - 1/2 tsp of garlic powder
- 1/4 tsp of salt
- 1/8 tsp of ground black pepper
- 1/2 tsp of smoked paprika
- 1/2 tsp of chili powder

Instructions

In a small bowl, add the breadcrumbs and red wine and mix to combine. Make tomato sauce. In a slow cooker, place all of the tomato sauce Ingredients and whisk to combine well. In a large bowl, place the ground pork and ground beef, mix. Add remaining meatball Ingredients and mix gently. Add the breadcrumb mixture and mix again. Divide the meatball mixture into 12 and roll gently into a ball. Add each meatball into the tomato sauce in a single layer in the slow cooker. Cover and cook on high for 4 hours or on low for 8 hours or until the meatballs are cooked. The cooked meatballs can remain on your slow cooker's "warm" setting for up to 2 hours. Turn the cooked meatballs over in the sauce to coat completely before serving.

Nutrients: kcal: 357, Fat: 23g, Total Carbs: 4g, Protein: 30g

23. BBQ Pork

Prep time: 10 minutes

Cook time: 7 hours

Servings: 9

Ingredients

For Pork

- 1 pound joint of pork
- 70 fl. oz of coke

For Sauce

- 0.22 pounds of tomato puree
- 0.044 pounds of brown sugar
- 1 tsp of garlic powder
- 2 tbsp of paprika
- 1 tbsp of white wine vinegar
- Salt and pepper to taste

Instructions

Add the joint to a slow cooker and pour over the coke. Cook on high heat if using a slow cooker for 5 hours. Shred the pork with a fork. Add the meat and juices into a container. Add the sauce ingredients to a container and stir to combine into a paste. Shred the meat. Add the shredded meat back into the slow cooker and pour the sauce over it. Cover the lid for around 40 minutes and stir occasionally.

Nutrients: Kcal: 357, Fat: 23g, Total Carbs: 4g, Protein: 30g

24. Chicken Tacos Queso

Prep time: 10 minutes

Cook time: 4 hours

Servings: 6

Ingredients

- 2 pounds of boneless skinless chicken breasts
- 10.5 oz. of Cream of Chicken Soup
- 7.5 oz. of chopped green chiles
- 3/4 cup of queso sauce
- 1/4 cup of salsa

Instructions

Add chicken, salsa, cream of chicken soup, and green chilis to the slow cooker. Stir Ingredients and cover the chicken with sauce. Cook on low for 4 hours or high for 2 1/2 hours. Remove liquid from the slow cooker and set aside. Shred Chicken. Add 3/4 cup of the queso sauce and reserved liquid until creaminess level desired. Stir and serve as tacos or rice bowls.

Nutrients: Kcal: 297, Fat: 11g, Total Carbs: 12g, Protein: 34g

25. Chicken Carbonara

Prep time: 10 minutes

Cook time: 4 hours

Servings: 4

Ingredients

- 7.5 oz. of Cream Cheese
- 2 tbsp of butter
- 2 pounds. of chicken thighs
- 16 oz. of mushrooms
- 3/4 cup of bacon, cooked and crumbled
- 1/4 cup of sweet peas

Instructions

Melt butter and cheese together. Whisk until smooth. Add chicken to slow cooker. Spread cheese mixture on top of chicken. Add mushrooms into the slow cooker. Once done, add bacon and peas. Stir together. Cook for an additional 10 minutes. Serve over gluten-free pasta, potatoes, or rice.

Nutrients: Kcal: 1159, Fat: 42g, Total Carbs: 8g, Protein: 44g

CHAPTER 7:

Side Dishes

1. Mashed Potatoes

Prep time: 10 minutes

Cook time: 3 hours 20 minutes

Servings: 8

Ingredients

- 4.96 pounds of potatoes
- 1 tbsp of minced garlic
- 4 Chicken stock cubes
- 7 fl. Oz of soured cream
- 0.49 pounds of cream cheese
- 0.26 pounds of butter
- Salt and pepper for seasoning

Instructions

Boil potatoes in a large bowl with garlic and stock. After 15 minutes, drain it out and mash it up in a bowl with sour cream and cream cheese. Transfer it into the slow cooker and cook on low for 3 hours. Before serving, add butter and seasoning salt and pepper.

Nutrients: Kcal: 430, Fat: 31g, Total Carbs: 31g, Protein: 15g

2. Baked Potatoes

Prep time: 15 minutes

Cook time: 4 hours 10 minutes

Servings: 4

Ingredients

- 4 potatoes for baking
- 1 tbsp of extra virgin olive oil
- 1 pinch of salt
- 4 pieces of aluminum sheet

Instructions

Prick the potatoes much time from a different direction. Rub them in olive oil. Wrap around the foil on them. Add in the slow cooker and cook on high for 4 hours. Or until tender.

Nutrients: Kcal: 240, Fat: 5g, Total Carbs: 50g, Protein: 8g

3. Wild Rice Mushrooms

Prep time: 10 minutes

Cook time: 7 hours

Servings: 12

Ingredients

- 8.11 fl. Oz. of water
- 6.7 fl. Oz. of beef stock
- 1 tin of French onion soup
- 0.28 pounds. of chopped mushrooms
- 0.2 pounds melted butter
- 0.44 pounds uncooked brown rice
- 0.24 pounds of uncooked wild rice

Instructions

In a slow cooker, add all the ingredients and stir well. Now cook on low for 7 hours or until rice tender.

Nutrients: Kcal: 234, Fat: 13g, Total Carbs: 22g, Protein: 6g

4. Carrots Glazed

Prep time: 10minutes

Cook time: 7 hours

Servings: 4

Ingredients

- 6 tbsp of orange marmalade
- 1.1 pounds of baby carrots
- 1 tbsp of water
- 0.077 pounds of butter
- Salt and pepper for seasoning

Instructions

Place all the ingredients into the slow cooker and stir well. Cook on low for 7 hours or until carrots are tender.

Nutrients: Kcal: 60, Fat: 1.5g, Total Carbs: 33g, Protein: 10g

5. Baked Haricot Beans

Prep time: 10 minutes

Cook time: 6 hours

Servings: 12

Ingredients

- 1.47 pounds of haricot beans
- 0.55 pounds of ham hocks
- 3 chopped onions
- 3tbsp of brown sugar
- 1 tsp of salt
- 7 fl. Oz. of water
- 7 tbsp of tomato ketchup
- 1 tbsp of tomato puree

Instructions

Boil the beans in the pan for 10 minutes. After heating, let it sit for 1 hour and drain it out of water. Add the beans to the slow cooker. Now add all the ingredients except for ketchup and puree and heat it for 5 hours with occasional stirring. In the final hour, add the ketchup and puree. Remove the hams from the hocks and discard the hocks. Mix well and then serve

Nutrients: Kcal: 151, Fat: 1.7g, Total Carbs: 21.6g, Protein: 18.3g

6. Baked Cannellini Bean

Prep time: 20 minutes

Cook time: 10 hours.

Servings: 12

Ingredients

- 1.43 pounds of Boiled cannellini beans
- 0.66 pounds tomato ketchup
- 10.55 fl. oz of water
- 5 tbsp of treacle
- 2 chopped onions
- 1 tbsp of mustard powder
- 1 tbsp of salt
- 6 chopped slices of bacon
- 0.44 pounds brown sugar

Instructions

Add all the ingredients onto the slow cooker. Cook on low for 10 hours with occasional stirring

Nutrients: Kcal: 200, Fat: 0.9g, Total Carbs: 50g, Protein: 35g

7. Sweetcorn

Prep time: 20 minutes

Cook time: 4 hours

Servings: 8

Ingredients

- 1.1 pounds of frozen sweetcorn
- 0.99 pounds of cubed cream cheese
- 5 tbsp of butter
- tbsp of water
- tbsp of sugar
- 0.49 pounds of grated cheddar cheese

Instructions

Add all the ingredients into the slow cooker and mix well. Cook on low for 4 hours or until cheese is melted. Stir well and serve hot!

Nutrients: Kcal; 120, Fat: 5g, Total Carbs: 20g, Protein: 5g

8. Cauliflower and Potato Mash

Prep time: 12 minutes

Cook time: 6 hours 10 minutes

Servings: 12

Ingredients

- 2.64 pounds peeled and cubed potatoes
- 8.44 fl. Oz. of chicken stock
- 1 chopped cauliflower
- 2.46 fl. Oz. of milk
- 0.132 pounds of butter
- 2.28 fl. Oz. of sour cream
- 1 tbsp of black pepper
- 1 tbsp of garlic powder
- 1/4 tbsp of paprika
- Salt for taste

Instructions

Add potatoes and chicken stock in the slow cooker and cook on low for 3 hours. Now add cauliflower and cook on low for more than 3 hours. Add in left ingredients and mix well. Mash the potatoes and cauliflower. Cook for more than 10 minutes and serve

Nutrients: Kcal: 136, Fat: 1g, Total Carbs: 29g, Protein: 4g

9. Spaghetti Squash

Prep time: 5 minutes

Cook time: 4 hours

Servings: 4

Ingredients

- 1 whole spaghetti squash
- 10.5 fl. Oz. of water

Instructions

Prick out the spaghetti squash about 15 times, add water and place in the slow cooker. Cook on low for 4 hours and then take it out for cooling for 10 minutes. Serve and enjoy

Nutrients: Kcal: 31, fat: 0.6g, Total Carbs: 7g, protein: 0.6g

10. Cheesy Potatoes

Prep time: 25 minutes

Cook time: 4 hours

Servings: 6

Ingredients

- 4 large potatoes thinly sliced
- 2 diced and sliced in rings onions
- 3 minced garlic cloves
- 0.66 pounds of cheese sauce
- 2 handful of grated cheese
- Salt and pepper for seasoning

Instructions

Take a bowl and mix onions and garlic. After oil spraying the slow cooker, add a single layer of potatoes on the base, then add garlic and onion. Keep layering till the ingredients last. Scatter cheese and season with salt and pepper. Cook on low heat for 4 hours until the potatoes are tender. Give a stir and serve

Nutrients: Kcal: 300, Fat: 19g, Total Carbs: 30g, Protein: 6g

11. Courgette

Prep time: 15 minutes

Cook time: 2hours

Servings: 4

Ingredients

- 1.5 pounds of sliced courgette
- 1 chopped red pepper
- 2 chopped garlic cloves
- 2 chopped onions
- Salt and pepper for taste
- 5 chopped plum tomatoes
- 2 tbsp of olive oil
- 1 handful of chopped basil

Instructions

Add all the ingredients into the slow cooker and cover the lid. Cook on high for 2 hours or until tender. Sprinkle basil before serving.

Nutrients: Kcal: 75, Fat: 4g, Total Carbs: 8g, Protein: 3g

12. Refried Pinto Beans

Prep time: 10 minutes

Cook time: 8 hours

Servings: 15

Ingredients

- 1 peeled and halved onion
- 1.27 pounds of pinto beans
- 1/2 fresh jalapeno chili pepper
- 2 tbsp of minced garlic
- 5 tbsp of salt
- 1 3/4 tsp of fresh black pepper
- 1/8 tsp of grounded cumin
- 70 fl. Oz. of water

Instructions

Add all the ingredients into the slow cooker. Cook on high for 8hours. Mash the beans when cooked and keep mashing till you get the desired consistency. Serve and enjoy!

Nutrients: Kcal: 384, Fat: 18g, Total Carbs: 40g, Protein: 14g

13. Pomegranate and Vanilla Brussels Sprout

Prep time: 10 minutes

Cook time: 2 hours

Servings: 8

Ingredients

- 2 pounds of halved Brussels sprouts
- 3 cups of chicken stock
- 2 cloves of minced garlic
- 1/4 cup of butter
- 2 tsp of vanilla bean paste
- 1 tsp of salt
- 1/2 tsp of black pepper
- Pomegranate Syrup
- 6 slices of crisp cooked bacon
- 1/4 cup of chopped toasted walnut

Instructions

Place Brussels sprouts in a slow cooker. Add garlic and broth. Cover and cook on high until they are tender and crisp. Turn off the cooker. Drain the sprout thoroughly and return to the slow cooker. In a small bowl, combine the next four ingredients till pepper and stir into sprouts. Drizzle with the pomegranate syrup and top with the bacon.

Nutrients: Kcal; 171, Fat: 10g, Total Carbs: 18g, Protein: 5g

14. Vegetable Mashup

Prep time: 20 minutes

Cook time: 3 hours

Servings: 8

Ingredients

- 12 oz. of halved and sliced zucchini
- 8 oz. of halved and sliced yellow summer squash
- 3 cups of fresh cremini mushrooms
- 2 red sweet peppers
- 2/3 cup of sliced leek
- 2 cloves of minced garlic
- 2 tbsp of chicken or vegetable broth
- 3 tbsp of Thai red curry paste
- 1/3 cup of coconut milk
- 1 tbsp of grated ginger
- 1/4 cup of shredded basil leaves

Instructions

In a slow cooker, combine all the ingredients except for broth and curry paste. In a small bowl, mix broth and curry paste; pour over vegetables. Cover and cook on low for 3 hours. Stir in coconut milk and ginger. Sprinkle with basil.

Nutrients: Kcal: 60, Fat: 2g, Total Carbs: 9g, Protein: 2g

15. Clapshot

Prep time: 15 minutes

Cook time: 3 hours

Servings: 4

Ingredients

- Salt for taste
- Onion
- Butter
- Chives
- 1.5 pounds Potatoes
- 1.5 pounds of Turnip

Instructions

Cut the vegetables into a cube and place them in salted water inside the slow cooker. Cook on high for about 3 hours. Make 1-inch cube slices of potatoes and place them in the slow cooker with other vegetables. Cook for about 3 more hours. With the vegetables. Place in a bowl and mix or beat until fully fluffy. Top it up with the butter and enjoy!

Nutrients: Kcal: 244, Fat: 1, Total Carbs: 45, Protein: 15

16. Peppered Bacon With Ranch Beans

Prep time: 25 minutes

Cook time: 6 hours

Servings: 20

Ingredients

- 9 slices of half-cut peppered bacon
- 1 cup of chopped onion
- 2/3 cup of chopped green sweet pepper
- 2 of the minced fresh jalapeño chili peppers
- 3 cloves of minced garlic
- 1 cup of stout beer
- 2 of 15-ounce cans of white beans
- 2 of 15-ounce cans of pinto beans
- 1 cup of the bottled barbecue sauce
- 1/2 cup of the packed brown sugar
- 1/2 cup of the apple cider vinegar
- 3 tbsp of the Worcestershire sauce
- 3 tbsp of mustard

Instructions

Cook bacon on a skillet on medium-low heat to remove fat but don't make it crisp. Chop off the 6 pieces of bacon and store the remaining. Store 1 tbsp Of dripping bacon from the skillet. Add in the chopped bacon, onion, jalapeño peppers, sweet pepper and garlic into the skillet. Cook over medium and high heat for 3 minutes. Scrape up the bits from the bottom of the pan. Now pour in the beer; simmer for 2 to 3 minutes. Transfer mixture slow cooker. Drain the white and pinto beans but without rinsing. Add in all the ingredients. Sprinkle stored bacon on top of the beans. Now cover with the lid and cook on a high setting for 4 hours. Beans should be tender.

Nutrients: Kcal: 167, Fat: 2g, Total Carbs: 30g, Protein: 7g

17. Stovies

Prep time: 20 minutes

Cook time: 4 hours

Servings: 4

Ingredients

- 2 onions
- 2.5 pounds of potatoes
- 1 tbsp of beef dripping
- 1 beef stock cube
- 1 tbsp of salt
- 2 tbsp of water

Instructions

Cut and slice the onions into medium-sized pieces. Take a pan and add the dripping. Now add the onions and slowly and gently stir them until they are soft and not brown colored. Add in the potatoes and mix evenly. Transfer all the material to the slow cooker. Add the left ingredients into the slow cooker and pour the water to get them socked just enough for slow cooking. Put the lid and heat at high for 1 hour and 20 minutes, then cook on low for the same time. Now take it out and rough the edges of the potatoes using a spoon. Serve and enjoy!

Nutrients: Kcal: 125, Fat: 12, Total Carbs: 36, Protein: 22

18. Orange Sage Sweet Potato With Bacon

Prep time: 15 minutes

Cook time: 5 hours

Servings: 10

Ingredients

- 4 pounds of peeled and sliced sweet potato
- 1/2 cup of frozen orange juice
- 3 tbsp of brown sugar
- 1 1/2 tsp of salt
- 1/2 tsp of crushed dried leaf sage
- 1/2 tsp of crushed dried thyme
- 2 tbsp of butter
- 4 slices of crispy and cooked bacon

Instructions

Add sweet potato slices slow cooker. Stir together all the ingredients in a small bowl and pour over the sweet potato in the slow cooker. Dot with butter. Cook on low-heat setting for 6 hours or on high setting for 2 and 1/2 hours. Sprinkle with bacon & serve!

Nutrients: Kcal: 190, Fat: 4g, Total Carbs: 36g, Protein: 4

19. Creamy Spinach

Prep time: 10 minutes

Cook time: 6 hours

Servings: 6

Ingredients

- 16 oz. of chopped and dry spinach
- 1 beaten egg
- 1 cup of ricotta cheese
- 4 oz. of cubed cream cheese
- 2 tbsp of butter
- 1 tbsp of finely chopped garlic
- 1/2 tbsp of salt
- 1/2 tbsp of grounded black pepper
- Red pepper flakes dash
- 1 cup of grated parmesan cheese

Instructions

Combine all the ingredients except for the parmesan cheese into the slow cooker and mix well. Now sprinkle the parmesan cheese over the material and cook on a low setting for 6 hours. Stir halfway through the process. Serve and enjoy!

Nutrients: Kcal: 305, Fat: 23g, Total Carbs: 8g, Protein: 18g

20. Cornbread And Sausage

Prep time: 15 minutes

Cook time: 4 hours

Servings: 8

Ingredients

- 4 tbsp of butter
- 1 cup of chopped onions
- 16 oz. of cornbread crumbs
- 8 oz. of grounded pork sausages
- 1 chopped celery
- 2 tbsp of chopped fresh parsley
- 1/2 tbsp of the rubbed sage
- 1 tsp of poultry seasoning
- 2 1/2 cup of chicken broth
- 1 beat egg
- 1/2 cup of dried cranberries

Instructions:

Spray the slow cooker with baking spray. In a large skillet, brown the sausage, add onions and celery and cook until vegetables become tender. Now add seasoning, parsley and sage in the skillet. In a large bowl, add sausage, vegetables, chicken broth, salt and pepper, blend well, and add the beaten egg; keep stirring while adding cranberries. Add it to the slow cooker, cook on high for 45 minutes, and then go to low and cook for 4 and half hours.

Nutrients: Kcal: 281, Fat: 16g, Total Carbs: 25g, Protein: 13g

21. Macaroni and Cheese

Prep time: 10 minutes

Cook time: 3 hours

Servings: 6

Ingredients

- 9 oz. of elbow macaroni
- 3 tbsp of extra virgin olive oil
- 2 tbsp of butter
- 1 1/2 cup of evaporating milk
- 1/2 tsp of the salt
- 1/4 tsp grounded black pepper
- 9 oz. cheddar cheese, shredded
- 4 tbsp of melted butter

Instructions

Boil macaroni and then drain them out by rinsing them with hot water. Spread the butter on all sides of the slow cooker until covered. Combine all the ingredients, including the boiled macaroni and blend them inside the slow cooker. Cover the lid and cook for 3 hours on low and stir gently. When the cheese is melted, take out the material and serve hot or as you desire!

Nutrients: Kcal: 510, Fat: 37g, Total Carbs: 20g, Protein: 25g

22. Creamy Chicken Peas With Mushrooms

Prep time: 10 minutes

Cook time: 2 hours 30 minutes

Servings: 6

Ingredients

- Salad dressing
- 1/4 cup of water
- 8 oz. of cream cheese
- 8 oz. of condensed cream of chicken soup
- 5 boneless and skinless chicken breasts
- 8 oz. pieces of mushrooms
- 1 cup of peas

Instructions

Grease the slow cooker and place the chicken in the bottom. Spread it evenly. Combine the salad and water in the bowl and evenly add in the slow cooker. Cover and cook for 2 and half hours on a high setting. Blend the cream cheese and soup in a bowl. Add mushrooms and peas in it and pour the mixture evenly on the chicken in the slow cooker. Now cook for more than 2 hours on a high setting. Stir and serve!

Nutrients: Kcal: 350, Fat: 25g, Total Carbs: 17g, Protein: 7g

23. Sweet and Tart Red Cabbage

Prep time: 20 minutes

Cook time: 8 hours

Servings: 6

Ingredients

- 1 shredded red cabbage
- 4 chopped onions
- 4 shredded and peeled apples
- 6.7 oz. of water
- 3 tbsp of brown sugar
- 6.5 oz. of vinegar
- 0.132 pounds of butter
- Salt for taste

Instructions

Combine all the ingredients in the slow cooker and cook on low for 8 hours by covering the lid. Take it out and serve

Nutrients: Kcal: 83.5, Fat: 4.7g, Total Carbs: 11.3g, Protein: 0.9g

24. Thanksgiving Stuffing

Prep time: 25 minutes

Cook time: 8 hours

Servings: 16

Ingredients

- 0.52 pounds of butter
- 0.7 pounds of chopped onions
- 0.5 pounds of chopped celery
- 4 tbsp of chopped parsley
- 0.77 pounds of bread cubes
- 1 tbsp of poultry seasoning
- 1 and 1/2 tsp of dried sage
- 1 tsp of dried thyme
- 1/2 tsp of marjoram
- 1 1/2 tsp of salt
- 1/2 tsp of grounded black pepper
- 35 fl. Oz. of chicken broth
- 2 beaten eggs

Instructions

In a frying pan, cook onions, celery, parsley and mushrooms over medium heat. Take a large mixing bowl and add in all the left ingredients one by one and mix them up. Transfer the material to the slow cooker and cover the lid. Cook for 8 hours on low heat. Serve and enjoy

Nutrients: Kcal: 252, Fat: 20g, Total Carbs: 30g, Protein: 8.5g

25. Cranberry Sauce

Prep time: 5 minutes

Cook time: 3 hours 45 minutes

Servings: 12

Ingredients

- 4.2 fl. Oz. of orange juice
- 0.22 pounds of brown sugar
- 1 can of fresh cranberries
- 4.2 fl. Oz. of water
- 0.22 pounds of caster sugar
- 1/4 tsp of cinnamon

Instructions

Combine all the ingredients in a slow cooker and stir. Cook on high for 3 hours. Stir in each hour. Keep on stirring until the sauce is thickened and most cranberries have popped in for about 45 minutes.

Nutrients: Kcal; 418, Fat: 0.4g, Total Carbs: 107g, Protein: 0.6g

CHAPTER 8:

Snack Recipes

1. Easy Chex Mix

Prep time: 10 minutes

Cook time: 3 hours

Servings: 12

Ingredients

- 74.9 oz of cups cereal
- 16.6 oz of pretzels
- 8.3 oz of cheerios
- 8.3 oz of peanuts
- 6 tbsp of butter
- 1 tbsp of salt
- 2.1 fl oz of Worcestershire sauce
- 1 tsp of garlic powder

Instructions

In a slow cooker bowl, combine cereal, pretzels, cheerios, and peanuts. Whisk together butter and seasoned salt in a separate basin until the salt is dissolved. Stir in the Worcestershire sauce until it is evenly distributed. Drizzle the sauce over the cereal mixture in an equal layer. Toss for about 1 minute or until the Ingredients are uniformly distributed. Cover and cook on low for about 3 hours, stirring once an hour, twice an hour, and once an hour and a half to ensure the mixture does not burn. Then, once the mixture has cooled to room temperature, spread it out evenly on a couple of baking sheets or parchment paper. Serve immediately or keep in an airtight jar for up to 3 weeks.

Nutrients: Kcal 130, Fat: 3.5g, Total Carbs: 23g, Protein: 2g

2. Crispy Chicken Taquitos

Prep time: 20 minutes

Cook time: 8 hours

Servings: 4

Ingredients

- 3-4 chicken breasts
- 8 oz of cream cheese
- 2.8 oz of jalapeños
- 1 tsp of garlic powder
- 1 tsp of salt
- 1 tsp of cumin
- 16 tortillas
- 12.5 oz of shredded cheese

Instructions

In a small saucepan, melt the butter and add the pineapple juice. Remove from the equation. On the bottom of the slow cooker, spread the crushed pineapple in a layer. Place the cherry pie filling on top of the pineapple in a uniform layer, and then pour the dry cake mix on top of the cherry filling in the slow cooker. Pour the butter and pineapple juice mixture over the dry cake mix, stirring to combine. Cook for about 3 hours on low in the slow cooker. Place the dessert on plates and set aside to cool for about 5 minutes before serving. Serve with a scoop of vanilla ice cream on the side.

Nutrients: Kcal 539, Fat: 33g, Total Carbs: 54g, Protein: 8g

3. Chicken Pita Bites

Prep time: 15 minutes

Cook time: 7 hours

Servings: 6

Ingredients

- 1 pound of boneless chicken thighs
- 1 onion
- 1 tbsp of ginger
- 1 tbsp of garlic
- 2 tbsp of cumin
- 1 tsp of cinnamon
- 2 tbsp paprika
- 12.5 fl oz of chicken stock
- 2 tbsp of lemon juice
- 4.2 oz of green olives
- Salt-to taste
- 3 tbsp of oil
- 6 pita breads
- 2 tbsp of hummus
- 1 tsp of parsley

Instructions

Heat the oil in a skillet and cook the onions with some salt and pepper until golden. Cook for another minute after adding the ginger and garlic. After that, add the cumin and cinnamon. Cook for a few minutes after thoroughly mixing. Place the chicken thighs in the slow cooker and pour the onion mixture over them. Combine the chicken stock, lemon juice, olives, salt, and pepper in a large mixing bowl. Allow it to cook on low for 6-7 hours, covered. When the chicken is done, shred it. Preheat oven to 350°F. Place the pita quarters on a baking pan and toast for about 10 minutes, or until crispy. Spread hummus on top, followed by chicken. Serve immediately, garnished with fresh parsley.

Nutrients: Kcal 486, Fat: 21g, Total Carbs: 73g, Protein: 4.9g

4. Beef Ranch And Cheesy Potatoes

Prep time: 15 minutes

Cook time: 8 hours

Servings: 8

Ingredients

- 6 slices of bacon
- 3 pounds of red potatoes
- 12.5 oz of cheddar cheese
- 1 tbsp of Ranch Seasoning
- 1 tbsp of salad dressing mix
- 2 tbsp of chives

Instructions

Preheat the oven to 400°F. Aluminum foil should be used to line a baking pan. Place the bacon in a single layer on the baking sheet that has been prepared. Place into oven and bake until brown and crispy, about 12-14 minutes. Allow to cool completely before disintegrating; set aside. Coat a slow cooker with nonstick spray and line it with aluminum foil, leaving enough overhang to wrap the potatoes on top. Fill the slow cooker with an even layer of potatoes. Repeat with cheese, Ranch Seasoning, and bacon, reserving cheese each time. Aluminum foil should be used to cover the potatoes. Cover and simmer for 7-8 hours on low heat or 3-4 hours on high heat, or until potatoes are soft. Lastly, top with the remaining cheese. Cook, covered, for about 1-2 minutes, or until the cheese has melted. Serve immediately with chives as a garnish.

Nutrients: Kcal 377.8, Fat: 16.3g, Total Carbs: 47.9g, Protein: 10.2g

5. Honey Pork

Prep time: 10 minutes

Cook time: 9 hours

Servings: 6

Ingredients

- 3 pounds of boneless pork
- 4.2 fl oz of honey
- 4.2 fl oz of vinegar
- 2.1 oz of blackberry jam
- 2.1 fl oz of hoisin sauce
- 4.2 fl oz of chicken broth
- 2 tsp of garlic
- 4.2 oz of onion
- 1 tbsp of cornstarch
- coleslaw
- 12 buns or rolls

Instructions

Trim the pork shoulder of any excess fat and place it in the slow cooker. Whisk the honey, vinegar, jam, chicken broth, garlic, and onion together in a medium bowl, then pour the sauce over the pork shoulder. Cover the slow cooker and simmer on low for about 8 to 9 hours, or until the pork shoulder is no longer pink and cooked through. Remove the pork shoulder from the slow cooker with tongs, retain the liquids, and set aside on a chopping board. Shred the pork shoulder with two forks into smaller pieces. In a large mixing bowl, place the pulled pork and serve with sauce and bun rolls.

Nutrients: Kcal 187.5, Fat: 6.1g, Total Carbs: 11.4g, Protein: 20.9g

6. Barbeque Kielbasa

Prep time: 20 minutes

Cook time: 4 minutes

Servings: 8

Ingredients

- 2 cups ketchup
- 4.2 oz of brown sugar
- 1 tbsp of Worcestershire sauce
- 2 tsp of mustard
- 1 tsp of hot sauce
- 1 onion
- 4.2 fl oz of bourbon
- 2 pounds of kielbasa

Instructions

Combine all Ingredients in the slow cooker. Cover and cook on low for about 4-5 hours, until sausage is hot.

Nutrients: Kcal 532, Fat: 33g, Total Carbs: 33g, Protein: 17g

7. Chicken Buffalo Meatballs

Prep time: 15 minutes

Cook time: 2 hours 5 minutes

Servings: 6

Ingredients

- 6.2 oz of panko
- 1 large egg
- 1/2 tsp of garlic powder
- 1/2 tsp of onion powder
- 2 green onions
- kosher salt, to taste
- black pepper, to taste
- 6.3 fl oz of buffalo sauce
- 11.5 oz of cheese dressing
- 1.1 oz of coconut

Instructions

Preheat the oven to 400°F. Set aside a baking sheet lined with parchment paper or a silicone baking mat. Combine ground chicken, panko, egg, garlic and onion powder, and green onions in a large mixing bowl; season to taste with salt and pepper. Stir with a wooden spoon or clean hands until everything is fully blended. Place the meatballs on the prepared baking sheet and bake for 4-5 minutes, or until golden brown on all sides. In a slow cooker, place the meatballs. Stir in the buffalo sauce and toss gently to mix. Cook for about 2 hours on low heat, covered. If desired, sprinkle with blue cheese dressing right before serving.

Nutrients: Kcal 273.2, Fat: 0.2g, Total Carbs: 23.1g, Protein: 15.5g

8. Chicken Wings

Prep time: 5 minutes

Cook time: 6 hours 5 minutes

Servings: 4

Ingredients

- 4.2 fl oz of soy sauce
- 4.2 fl oz of vinegar
- 3 tbsp of honey
- 1 tsp of garlic
- 1 tsp of sriracha sauce
- 1 tsp of ginger powder
- 3 tbsp of lime juice
- Zest of one lime
- 2 pounds of chicken wings
- 4 tsp of cornstarch
- 2 tsp of sesame seeds
- 2 tbsp of chopped chives

Instructions

Grease your slow cooker generously with butter or margarine. Pour the milk, sugar, eggs, and vanilla extract into a mixing bowl and thoroughly combine everything. Spread butter or margarine on both sides of your hot cross bun bread slices. Make sure each slice of bun loaf is well covered in the milk mixture. In your slow cooker, layer each slice. Cook the pudding for about 4 hours on low. Take off the cover of the slow cooker and place it in an oven at 392°F for no more than 20 minutes to obtain a golden crisp to the top slices, or enjoy it straight from the slow cooker. Serve it plain, with custard, cream, or ice cream.

Nutrients: Kcal 362, Fat: 20g, Total Carbs: 20g, Protein: 23g

9. Barbeque Small Smokies

Prep time: 5 minutes

Cook time: 2 hours

Servings: 8

Ingredients

- 16.7 fl oz of tomato ketchup
- 12.5 oz of brown sugar
- 4.2 onion
- 2 13 oz of smokies
- 1 tsp of green onions

Instructions

In a slow cooker, combine the ketchup, liquid smoke, brown sugar, and onion. To blend, stir everything together. Stir in the smokies until everything is evenly coated. Cook on high for about 2 hours or low for about 3 hours, covered in the slow cooker. Set the slow cooker to warm and serve immediately, garnished with chopped green onions.

Nutrients: Kcal 240, Fat: 15g, Total Carbs: 163g, Protein: 9g

10. Mozzarella Meatballs

Prep time: 15 minutes

Cook time: 3 hours

Servings: 4

Ingredients

- 1 pound of ground beef
- 8.3 oz of bread crumbs
- 1 egg
- 1 egg yolk
- 1 tsp of minced garlic
- 1 tsp of onion powder
- 1 tbsp of Italian seasoning
- 1 tsp of salt
- 1/2 tsp of black pepper
- 3-4 mozzarella cheese sticks
- 4 tbsp of alfredo sauce

Instructions

Each cheese stick should be cut into pieces. Place on a plate and chill until ready to use in the freezer. Combine the ground beef, bread crumbs, egg and yolk, garlic, onion powder, Italian seasoning, and salt and pepper in a mixing bowl. Scoop the meat mixture and roll it into a ball. Gently press a slice of cooled mozzarella into the meatball's center. To cover the hole where the mozzarella cheese was placed, roll the ball in your palms. Repeat with the remaining meat and cheese in a greased slow cooker. Cover and simmer on high for about 1-2 hours or low for around 3-4 hours until meat is cooked through in the slow cooker. It's fine if the cheese starts to melt out of the meatballs. Garnish with a pinch of fresh chopped parsley or dry Italian seasoning, if desired. For dipping, serve with marinara or Alfredo sauce.

Nutrients: Kcal 492, Fat: 31g, Total Carbs: 22g, Protein: 30g

11. Creamy Cheese Chicken Taquitos

Prep time: 15 minutes

Cook time: 4 hours

Servings: 4

Ingredients

- 1 tsp of garlic powder
- 2 boneless chicken breasts
- 1 tsp of chili powder
- 1 tsp of cumin
- 8 oz of cream cheese
- 2.8 fl oz of water
- 4.2 oz of cheese
- 12 tortillas
- salt to taste
- pepper to taste
- 1 tsp of cilantro
- 1 tsp of salsa
- 1 tsp of sour cream

Instructions

Combine the chicken, spices, cheese and water in a slow cooker. Cook on low mode for around 7 hours, covered. Remove chicken from the slow cooker minutes before serving, shred using a fork, and return to the cooker. Allow it to simmer for another 15 minutes. Preheat the oven to 400°F. Fill each tortilla with about a quarter cup of the chicken mixture. Sprinkle cheese over on top. Roll tightly and place on a prepared baking sheet in a single layer. Bake for 10 minutes, or until shredded cheese is melted and tortillas are slightly browned. Serve with the toppings and sauces of your choice.

Nutrients: Kcal 574, Fat: 30g, Total Carbs: 50g, Protein: 26g

12. Spicy Meatballs

Prep time: 5 minutes

Cook time: 4 hours

Servings: 12

Ingredients

- 8.3 oz of raspberry
- 1 1/2 pound of frozen meatballs
- 12 oz of sweet chili sauce
- 1 tsp of green onions

Instructions

In a slow cooker, place the meatballs. Combine the sauce and raspberry in a mixing bowl and pour over the meatballs. To blend, stir everything together. Cook on low mode for about 6 hours, covered. Serve immediately with a sprinkling of chopped green onions.

Nutrients: Kcal 286, Fat: 12g, Total Carbs: 34g, Protein: 10g

13. Pork Tacos

Prep time: 10 minutes

Cook time: 4 hours

Servings: 6

Ingredients

- 4 pounds of boneless pork
- salt to taste
- 8.3 oz of salsa
- 8 oz of chipotle chili
- 1 tbsp of ground cumin
- 1 tbsp of smoked paprika
- 3 tsp of minced garlic
- 1 small onion
- 10 tortillas

Instructions

Trim the pork of any excess fat and cut it into four pieces. Season generously with salt on all sides. Combine all the sauces and spices in a slow cooker. Turn the pork and onion in the slow cooker to coat them in the sauce. Cook for around 6-8 hours on low or about 4 hours on high. To shred the pork, place it in a bowl and use two forks to shred it. If desired, drain the sauce and skim off the fat with a spoon or a fat separator. Toss the pork with just enough sauce to keep it moist. Warm the tortillas before filling them with pulled pork and preferred decorations.

Nutrients: Kcal 304, Fat: 14g, Total Carbs: 7g, Protein: 37g

14. Garlic Shrimps

Prep time: 15 minutes

Cook time: 1 hour

Servings: 5

Ingredients

For the Creole Seasoning

- 1 tbsp of paprika - 1 tbsp of salt
- 1 tbsp of garlic powder
- 2 tsp of black pepper
- 1 tsp of onion powder
- 1 tsp of cayenne pepper
- 1 tsp of dried oregano
- 1 tsp of dried thyme

For the Garlic Shrimp

- 4 tbsp of butter
- 2.1 fl oz of olive oil - 5 tsp of garlic
- 1 tsp of Creole seasoning
- 1/4 tsp of black pepper
- 1/8 tsp of cayenne pepper
- 1 1/2 pounds of extra-large shrimp
- 2 tbsp of parsley

Instructions

Collect the necessary components. Combine all of the ingredients in a mixing bowl and stir until well combined. In a mixing dish, combine all of the seasonings. Set aside spice and store the rest, covered, in a cool, dark place. In a slow cooker, combine the butter, oil, chopped garlic, Creole spice, and black and cayenne peppers. Combine garlic and butter in a mixing bowl. Cook on high for about 25 to 30 minutes, covered. Cook on high, covered. Peel the shrimp in the meantime. Cut the back of each shrimp with a small, sharp knife. Add the prepped shrimp and toss to coat them in the oil and butter mixture in the slow cooker. Add the shrimp that have been prepared. Cook, covered, for about 20 to 30 minutes on high, stirring halfway through the cooking time. Cover and cook on high for 30 minutes. Pour the sauce over them and transfer them to a serving dish. Transfer to a serving platter. Garnish with fresh chopped parsley if desired.

Nutrients: Kcal 246, Fat: 13g, Total Carbs: 6g, Protein: 27g

15. Ham Balls

Prep time: 15 minutes

Cook time: 3 hours

Servings: 15

Ingredients

- 1 pound of ham
- 1 pound of pork
- 8.3 oz of breadcrumbs
- 2 eggs
- 4.2 fl oz of cup milk
- 2 tbsp of parsley

For the Glaze

- 12.5 fl oz of ketchup
- 12 oz brown sugar
- 4.2 fl oz of apple cider vinegar
- 2 tsp of mustard powder

Instructions

Preheat oven to 350°F. Using nonstick cooking spray, coat a baking pan. Milk, ham, pork, breadcrumbs, eggs, and parsley, if used, should all be mixed. Mix until everything is well combined. Combine the ham, pork, breadcrumbs, beaten eggs, milk, and parsley in a mixing dish. Make meatballs out of the mixture. Place the ham balls in the baking tray that has been prepared and bake for about 45 minutes. Meatballs made of ham in a casserole dish. Meanwhile, in a saucepan, combine the ketchup, brown sugar, vinegar, and powdered mustard. Bring the pan to a low simmer over medium heat.

Nutrients: Kcal 283, Fat: 9g, Total Carbs: 31g, Protein: 18g

16. Mashed Potatoes

Prep time: 25 minutes

Cook time: 3 hours 35 minutes

Servings: 30

Ingredients

- 5 pounds of potatoes
- 8 oz of cream cheese
- 8.3 fl oz of sour cream
- 1 tsp of onion powder
- 1 1/2 tsp of salt
- 1/4 tsp of garlic powder
- 1/4 tsp of white pepper
- 1 large egg
- 2.8 oz of unsalted butter

Instructions

Collect the necessary components. Ingredients for mashed potatoes in a slow cooker Cook the potatoes until cooked in a large saucepan of boiling salted water, about 20 to 30 minutes. Potatoes should be cooked slowly. Mash the potatoes until no lumps remain. Combine the cream cheese, sour cream, onion powder, salt, pepper, and the egg in a large mixing bowl. In a greased baking dish, place the mashed potatoes. Butter should be melted and drizzled over the potatoes. Allow it to cool for about 20 minutes before covering and storing in the refrigerator for up to three days.

Nutrients: Kcal 339, Fat: 16g, Total Carbs: 43g, Protein: 7g

17. Nuts Cereal Mix

Prep time: 10 minutes

Cook time: 4 hours

Servings: 16

Ingredients

- 16.7 oz of wheat cereal
- 16.7 oz of corn cereal
- 16.7 oz of rice cereal
- 25 oz of thin pretzel sticks
- 13 oz of salted and mixed nuts
- 1 tsp of garlic salt
- 1 tsp of celery salt
- 1/2 tsp of seasoned salt
- 2 tbsp of cheese
- 2.8 fl oz of butter
- 2.8 fl oz of Worcestershire sauce

Instructions

Combine cereals, pretzels and nuts, as well as garlic salt, celery salt, seasoned salt, and grated Parmesan cheese, in a big paper bag. Empty the bag's contents into a large mixing basin and stir in the melted butter and Worcestershire sauce carefully with your hands. Fill the slow cooker with the contents of the bowl and simmer on low for about 3 to 4 hours. Spread the hot snack mixture onto the torn open bags and set aside to dry for at least an hour, allowing the paper to absorb any extra moisture. Serve immediately or keep in an airtight container.

Nutrients: Kcal 267, Fat: 16g, Total Carbs: 26g, Protein: 8g

18. Boiled Nuts

Prep time: 10 minutes

Cook time: 7 hours

Servings: 6

Ingredients

- 48 oz of raw shell peanuts
- 4.2 oz of salt
- 21.1 fl oz of water

Instructions

Fill a colander halfway with water and wash the peanuts until the water runs clear. In a slow cooker, combine the cleaned peanuts, salt, and water. Cover and stir well. Cook for roughly about 5 to 7 hours on high. Add extra water if necessary to keep the peanuts submerged in liquid. Drain the water gently and lay the peanuts in a colander in the skink to enable any remaining moisture to soak away.

Nutrients: Kcal 828, Fat: 72g, Total Carbs: 24g, Protein: 38g

19. Spicy Drumsticks

Prep time: 5 minutes

Cook time: 3 hours 30 minutes

Servings: 6

Ingredients

- 1 tbsp of creole seasoning
- 3 tbsp of brown sugar
- 1/2 tsp of salt
- 1/2 tsp of black pepper
- 4 tbsp of butter
- 10 chicken drumsticks

Instructions

Combine the brown sugar, salt, pepper, and melted butter with the Cajun or Creole spice. Arrange the drumsticks in the bottom of the slow cooker and season with the spice and butter mixture all over. Cook for roughly about 2 hours on high, covered. Drain any extra fluids, turn the chicken, and cook for another 2 hours on high, or until the chicken is browned and the juices are clear. Serve

Nutrients: Kcal 623, Fat: 38g, Total Carbs: 7g, Protein: 60g

20. Chicken Lettuce Cups

Prep time: 15 minutes

Cook time: 7 hours

Servings: 4

Ingredients

- 2 oz of brown sugar
- 2 fl oz of vinegar
- 1 tbsp of soy sauce
- 1 tbsp of ginger - 2 tbsp of garlic
- 1/4 tsp of red pepper
- 2 pounds of boneless, skinless chicken thighs
- 6.1 oz of white rice
- 1 orange - 2 scallions
- 1 small lettuce

Instructions

In a slow cooker, combine the sugar, vinegar, soy sauce, ginger, garlic, and red pepper. Turn the chicken to cover it in the sauce. Cook, covered, for about 6 to 7 hours on low or around 3 to 4 hours on high, until the chicken is cooked through and extremely tender. Meanwhile, peel the orange and remove the white pith. Place the orange in a medium bowl and cut it into thin half-moons. Add the scallions and fold them in. Shred the chicken into medium pieces with two forks and stir into the cooking liquid. Fill lettuce leaves halfway with rice, then top with chicken and orange mixture. Cook the rice for about 25 minutes before serving.

Nutrients: Kcal 438, Fat: 13g, Total Carbs: 30g, Protein: 47g

21. Warm Baked Potatoes

Prep time: 5 minutes

Cook time: 5 hours

Servings: 4

Ingredients

- 4 potatoes
- 1 tbsp of olive oil

Instructions

Each potato should be carefully washed and dried. Put the potatoes in a basin and prick them all over with a fork. Rub olive oil all over the potatoes to evenly coat them. Toss to coat and season with salt and pepper. Wrap each potato in foil and place it in a slow cooker pan in a single, even layer if feasible. Cook on high for about 4 hours for medium potatoes or about 5 hours for large potatoes, rotating the potatoes halfway during the cooking period. Insert a cutlery knife into the center of the potato, through the foil, to see whether it is done; it should easily glide in. Using a large spoon, carefully lift the potatoes from the slow cooker onto a plate or board. Serve your slow cooker jacket potatoes with the toppings of your choosing.

Nutrients: Kcal 224, Fat: 0.1g, Total Carbs: 37g, Protein: 4g

22. Tender and Delicious Sausages

Prep time: 10 minutes

Cook time: 8 hours 15 minutes

Servings: 6

Ingredients

- 1 tbsp of olive oil
- 12 sausages
- 8-10 bacon
- 1 onion
- 1 carrot
- 1 celery stalk
- 2 tbsp of garlic
- 3.4 fl oz of white wine
- 2 tbsp of tomato sauce
- 2 tsp of thyme leaves
- 1 tsp of oregano
- 14.1 oz of tin tomatoes
- 14.1 oz of tin butter beans
- 14.1 oz of borlotti beans
- 1 tsp of paprika
- 11.8 fl oz of chicken stock
- crusty bread

Instructions

Heat a little oil in a large frying pan, then fry the sausages and bacon on high until golden all over. Set aside and fry the vegetables and garlic together in the same way, very quickly. Before they are ready, pour in the white wine and scrape the bottom of the pan to get all the flavor. Pour the contents of the pan into a slow cooker. Add the meat and the remaining ingredients. Mix well and season. Cook for about 8 hours on low. Serve with big chunks of crusty bread.

Nutrients: Kcal 200, Fat: 8g, Total Carbs: 27g, Protein: 5g

23. Spicy Chicken Wings With Cheese Dip

Prep time: 30 minutes

Cook time: 3 hours

Servings: 8

Ingredients

For the Marinade

- 8 tsp of garlic - 2 tsp of thyme
- 2 tsp of chili flakes
- 1 lemon - 1 tbsp of brown sugar
- 1.4 oz of sea salt

For the Chicken Wings

- 40 chicken wings
- 33.8 fl oz of rapeseed oil

For the Spice Rub

- 2 tbsp of garlic salt - 1 tbsp of thyme leaves
- 1 tsp of cayenne pepper

For the Blue Cheese Dip

- 10.1 fl oz of soured cream
- 3.5 oz of cheese
- 2 tsp of garlic - 1/2 lemon
- 1/2 tsp of smoked paprika

Instructions

Place marinade ingredients in a large plastic bag and give it a shake until well combined. Put the chicken wings into the bag and rub until they are completely coated. Seal and chill for at least 8 hours. When the wings are marinated, preheat the oven to 302°F. Take the wings out of the marinade, wiping off as much as possible. Place the wings in a large, deep baking tray and pour over the oil to completely cover the wings. Top with foil and bake in the bottom of the oven for about 2 1/2 hours. Once wings are cooked, remove from the oil and drain well on a wire rack. Preheat grill to medium and grill wings for around 5-10 minutes, occasionally turning until crispy and golden. Combine the spice rub in a large bowl when the wings are ready, tip straight into the bowl until they are lightly dusted. Shake off any excess rub and lay on a large platter. Combine all the ingredients for the dip. Serve in a bowl with the wings.

Nutrients: Kcal 614, Fat: 12g, Total Carbs: 71g, Protein: 4.9g

24. Beef And Parmesan Dumplings

Prep time: 25 minutes

Cook time: 2 hours 20 minutes

Servings: 6

Ingredients

For the Beef Stew

- 7 oz of lambs' kidneys
- 3 tbsp olive oil
- 1 pound of beef joint
- 11 oz of shallots
- 20 oz of carrots - 2 tsp of garlic
- 3 tbsp of plain flour
- 1 tbsp of Worcestershire sauce
- 14 fl oz ale - 8 fl oz beef stock
- 6 tsp of thyme

For the Dumplings

- 1.8 oz of butter - 3.5 oz of flour
- 1.5 oz of Parmesan
- 4 tbsp of milk - 1 tbsp of thyme

Instructions

Whisk together the yolks, sugar, salt, and vanilla extract in a mixing bowl, then slowly whisk in the cream. Fill the slow cooker halfway up the sides of the ramekins with water. Fill ramekins halfway with custard. Cook on Low for about 2 hours, or until the custard is set but still jiggles slightly. Allow about 45 minutes for ramekins to cool completely on a rack. Chill the custards for at least 3 hours, uncovered. Serve immediately after browning the sugar. Return the beef and its juices to the pan, along with the Worcestershire sauce, ale, stock and thyme, stir until combined and bring to a boil. Cover with a lid and place in the oven for 2 hours, until the meat is tender. To make the dumplings, rub the butter into the flour until it resembles fine breadcrumbs. Stir through the Parmesan and add the milk. Mix with a knife to bring them together, then shape them into small balls. Remove the lid from the casserole dish and place the dumplings on the top. Return to the oven and cook for about 20 minutes until the dumplings are golden brown and cooked through. Garnish with the thyme leaves.

Nutrients: Kcal 495, Fat: 1.6g, Total Carbs: 17.5g, Protein: 4.4g

25. Delicious Stuffed Peppers

Prep time: 12 minutes

Cook time: 3 hours 30 minutes

Servings: 4

Ingredients

- 1 tbsp olive oil
- 1 red onion
- 9 oz of mushrooms
- 2.6 oz of kale
- 6.3 oz of chestnuts
- 2.6 oz of feta
- 1 tsp of oregano
- 4 red peppers

For the Pesto

- 1.8 oz of watercress
- 1.1 oz of walnut pieces
- 0.8 oz of hazelnuts
- 3.4 fl oz of olive oil
- 1/2 lemon

Instructions

Heat the oil over medium heat in a large frying pan and sauté the onion for about 3-4 minutes, until softened. Cook for another 4-5 minutes, or until the mushrooms have softened. Stir in the kale for 1 minute or until it begins to wilt. Remove the pan from the heat and toss in the chestnuts, mashing them with a fork in the pan. Combine the crumbled feta and oregano in a large mixing bowl. Season with salt and pepper to taste. Remove the pepper tops and set them aside. After seeding the peppers, divide the mushroom and chestnut mixture evenly and press it into the hollow. Replace the tops of the peppers in the slow cooker's dish. Set the slow cooker to low and simmer for about 5 to 6 hours, or until the peppers are tender.

Nutrients: Kcal 549, Fat: 24g, Total Carbs: 30g, Protein: 29g

CHAPTER 9:

Dessert Recipes

1. Rice Pudding

Prep time: 10 minutes

Cook time: 5 hours

Servings: 4

Ingredients

- 4 oz of rice pudding
- 2 oz of sugar
- 1 oz of margarine
- 40 oz of milk
- 1/2 tsp of cinnamon

Instructions

Put everything in the slow cooker, mix it, and set it to high. After approximately an hour, stir it again, then set it aside to continue cooking. To taste, add jam, syrup, or honey. Serve.

Nutrients: Kcal 111, Fat: 1.6g, Total Carbs: 21g, Protein: 3.3g

2. Black Forest Cake

Prep time: 5 minutes

Cook time: 3 hours

Servings: 10

Ingredients

- 4.2 oz of butter
- 15 oz of pineapple
- 17.6 oz of cherry pie filling
- 17.6 oz of chocolate cake mix

Instructions

In a small saucepan, melt the butter and add the pineapple juice. Remove from the equation. On the bottom of the slow cooker, spread the crushed pineapple in a layer. Place the cherry pie filling on top of the pineapple in a uniform layer, and then pour the dry cake mix on top of the cherry filling in the slow cooker. Pour the butter and pineapple juice mixture over the dry cake mix, stirring to combine. Cook for about 3 hours on low in the slow cooker. Place the dessert on plates and set aside to cool for about 5 minutes before serving. Serve with a scoop of vanilla ice cream on the side.

Nutrients: Kcal 539, Fat: 33g, Total Carbs: 54g, Protein: 8g

3. Apple Pudding

Prep time: 15 minutes

Cook time: 3 hours

Servings: 6

Ingredients

- 12.8 oz of apples
- 10 slices of bread, cubed
- 1/2 tsp of ground cinnamon
- 1/2 tsp of nutmeg
- Salt to taste
- 3.5 oz of brown sugar
- 4.6 oz of melted butter

Instructions

Place the apples in the slow cooker pot. Toss the bread cubes with the cinnamon, nutmeg, salt, and brown sugar in a medium mixing basin. Drizzle with melted butter and place on top of the apples. Cook on low for around 3 hours or until apples are soft, covered.

Nutrients: Kcal 486, Fat: 21g, Total Carbs: 73g, Protein: 4.9g

4. Chocolate Cake

Prep time: 15 minutes

Cook time: 6 hours

Servings: 16

Ingredients

- 17.6 oz of chocolate cake mix
- 1 pack of chocolate dessert mix
- 15.9 oz of soured cream
- 4 eggs
- 8.55 fl oz of water
- 6.1 fl oz of vegetable oil
- 5.6 oz of chocolate chips

Instructions

Combine cake mix and pudding mix in a large mixing basin. In the center, make a well and pour in the soured cream, eggs, water, and oil. Mix thoroughly or beat on low speed until well combined. Scrape down the sides of the bowl and mix thoroughly again, or beat for another 4 minutes on medium speed. Add the chocolate chips and mix well. Pour the batter into a slow cooker pot sprayed with nonstick cooking spray. Cook on low for about 6 hours, covered. Pour into individual serving bowls and serve.

Nutrients: Kcal 371, Fat: 15g, Total Carbs: 53g, Protein: 5g

5. Apple Crisp

Prep time: 30 minutes

Cook time: 3 hours

Servings: 6

Ingredients

For the Crisp

- 4.4 oz of flour
- 3.4 oz of caster sugar
- 1/4 tsp of nutmeg
- Salt to taste
- 4.23 oz of butter
- 3.38 oz of brown sugar
- 4.2 oz of walnuts
- 1/2 tsp of cinnamon

For Apples

- 2.1 oz of caster sugar
- 1 tbsp of cornflour
- 1/2 tsp of ginger
- 1/2 tsp of cinnamon
- 25.5 oz of cooking apples
- 2 tbsp of lemon juice

Instructions

In a mixing bowl, combine all the dry ingredients. Combine the butter and flour mixture until coarse crumbs form. Set aside after adding the walnuts. Combine cinnamon, sugar, cornstarch and ginger in a mixing bowl. Toss the apples with the cornflour mixture and lemon juice in a slow cooker. On top, sprinkle the walnut crumble topping. Cook for about 2 hours on high or around 4 hours on low until apples are soft. Cover the slow cooker partially for about 1 hour to let the topping firm. Then Serve.

Nutrients: Kcal 161, Fat: 3.4g, Total Carbs: 31g, Protein: 1.8g

6. Orange Sponge Chocolate Pudding

Prep time: 20 minutes

Cook time: 1 hour 30 minutes

Servings: 6

Ingredients

- 9.7 oz of caster sugar
- 9.7 oz of butter, softened
- 3 eggs
- 2 tbsp of milk
- 1/2 tsp of vanilla extract
- 2 oranges
- 2 tbsp of liqueur
- 9.7 oz of flour
- 1.2 oz of cocoa powder
- 1 tsp of baking powder

Instructions

Preheat the slow cooker on its highest setting. Grease six dishes with cooking spray. Combine the sugar and butter in a mixing bowl and beat until light and creamy. Combine the milk and vanilla essence in a mixing bowl. Mix in the orange zest and liqueur well. Combine the flour, cocoa powder, and baking powder in a mixing bowl and stir until well combined. Fill the dishes halfway with the mixture. Place the dishes in the preheated slow cooker over four layers of greaseproof paper and add in enough boiling water to cover them halfway. Cook for about 90 minutes with the lid on. Remove the paper and foil from the molds and remove them from the water bath. Invert onto a serving platter and tap out gently. Serve immediately.

Nutrients: Kcal 286, Fat: 13.5g, Total Carbs: 36.3g, Protein: 3.5g

7. Banana Foster

Prep time: 10 minutes

Cook time: 2 hours

Servings: 4

Ingredients

- 4 bananas
- 4 tbsp of butter
- 7.8 oz of brown sugar
- 4 tbsp of rum
- 1 tsp of vanilla extract
- 1/2 tsp of cinnamon
- 1.1 oz of walnuts
- 1.1 oz of coconut

Instructions

In the bottom of a slow cooker, layer sliced bananas. Combine butter, brown sugar, rum, vanilla, and cinnamon in a separate dish and pour over bananas. Cook for around 2 hours on low, covered. During the last 30 minutes of cooking, top bananas with walnuts and coconut.

Nutrients: Kcal 310, Fat: 8.6g, Total Carbs: 36g, Protein: 3.2g

8. Warm Cross Bun Loaf Pudding

Prep time: 15 minutes

Cook time: 4 hours

Servings: 4

Ingredients

- 13.5 fl oz of milk
- 3 tbsp of brown sugar
- 2 large eggs
- 1 tsp of vanilla extract
- 10 slices of bun loaf
- 3.5 oz of butter

Instructions

Grease your slow cooker generously with butter or margarine. Pour the milk, sugar, eggs, and vanilla extract into a mixing bowl and thoroughly combine everything. Spread butter or margarine on both sides of your hot cross bun bread slices. Make sure each slice of bun loaf is well covered in the milk mixture. In your slow cooker, layer each slice. Cook the pudding for about 4 hours on low. Take off the cover of the slow cooker and place it in an oven at 392°F for no more than 20 minutes to obtain a golden crisp to the top slices, or enjoy it straight from the slow cooker. Serve it plain, with custard, cream, or ice cream!

Nutrients: Kcal 90, Fat: 45g, Total Carbs: 6g, Protein: 6g

9. Peanut Butter Cake

Prep time: 15 minutes

Cook time: 1 hour 45 minutes

Servings: 8

Ingredients

- 7.1 oz of flour
- 3.5 oz of brown sugar
- 1 tsp of baking powder
- 1 tsp of soda
- 1/4 tsp of salt
- 8.8 oz of peanut butter
- 6.2 oz of soured cream
- 3 tbsp of butter
- 2 tbsp of boiling water
- 6.2 oz of dark chocolate chips
- 5.3 oz of caster sugar
- 6 tbsp of cocoa powder
- 6.1 fl oz of whole milk
- 1 tsp vanilla extract

Instructions

In a mixing bowl, combine all the dry ingredients. In a large mixing basin, combine peanut butter, soured cream, butter, and boiling water. Mix until thick paste forms. Stir the flour mixture into the peanut butter mixture until smooth, then fold in the chocolate chips. Grease the dish of your slow cooker generously and pour in the cake Ingredients. Whisk together the caster sugar, cocoa powder, milk, and vanilla extract in a small bowl until smooth. Pour over the cake in the slow cooker. Cover and cook for about 1 to 2 hours, or until the sides of the cake begin to peel away from the sides of the ceramic dish and seem solid. Serve.

Nutrients: Kcal 437, Fat: 20.6g, Total Carbs: 59.13g, Protein: 5.92g

10. Berries Compote

Prep time: 10 minutes

Cook time: 1 hour 35 minutes

Servings: 4

Ingredients

- 30 oz of frozen mixed berries
- 3.5 oz of caster sugar
- 2 tsp of orange zest
- 2 fl oz of orange juice
- 2 tbsp of cornflour
- 2 tbsp of water

Instructions

In a slow cooker, combine the berries, sugar, zest, and juice. Cook for about 2 hours on high, or until bubbling. In a cup, whisk together cornflour and water until completely dissolved. Add to the berry mixture and combine well. Cook for another 5 to 10 minutes, covered until the sauce has thickened. Serve it warm or at room temperature is fine.

Nutrients: Kcal 466, Fat: 19.g, Total Carbs: 79.1g, Protein: 5.4g

11. Cinnamon Rolls

Prep time: 30 minutes

Cook time: 2 hours

Servings: 10

Ingredients

- 25 fl oz of milk
- 2 tsp of Yeast - 2.1 oz of sugar
- 1 tsp of sugar - 3/4 tsp of salt
- 4 tbsp of unsalted butter
- 1 large egg
- 23 oz of all-purpose flour

For Filling

- 5 tbsp of unsalted butter
- 1 tbsp of cinnamon
- 2.8 oz of granulated sugar

For Icing

- 10.4 oz of confectioners' sugar
- 2 tbsp of maple syrup - 2 tbsp of milk

Instructions

Warm the milk in the microwave or on the stove over low heat until it is lukewarm. In the bowl of a stand mixer fitted with the dough hook or paddle attachment, pour the heated milk. Sugar and yeast, whisked in cover with a clean towel and set aside for about 5-10 minutes, or until the yeast has foamed. Mix the remaining sugar, salt, butter, egg, and flour on low speed until mixed. Using a low-speed mixer, gradually add the remaining flour until a soft dough forms. Allow the dough to rest for about 10 minutes. Line slow cooker with greased parchment paper during these 10 minutes. Roll out the dough into a rectangle after 10 minutes. On top, spread the softened butter. Combine the cinnamon and sugar, then sprinkle over the butter. Roll out the dough tightly, then cut it into 10-12 even pieces and lay them in the slow cooker lined with parchment paper. Cook for 2 hours on high, or until the rolls are fully cooked through, in your slow cooker. Garnish your cinnamon rolls with glaze just before serving. Combine the confectioners' sugar, maple syrup, and milk in a mixing bowl and whisk until smooth. If the sauce is too thick, add a bit more milk. Drizzle the sauce over the hot rolls. Keep in the refrigerator overnight and reheat as desired.

Nutrients: Kcal 290, Fat: 9.9g, Total Carbs: 47g, Protein: 3.8g

12. Blackberry Cobbler

Prep time: 15 minutes

Cook time: 2 hours

Servings: 8

Ingredients

For the Blackberry layer

- 41.2 oz of blackberries
- 1 tbsp of cornstarch
- 2 tbsp of salted butter
- 2.1 oz of sugar

For the Cobbler layer

- 10.4 oz of flour
- 6.2 oz of sugar
- 1 1/2 tsp of baking powder
- 1/2 tsp of salt
- 8.3 fl oz of milk
- 1 tsp of vanilla extract
- 2 tbsp of salted butter

For the Topping

- 1 tbsp of sugar
- 1/4 tsp of cinnamon

Instructions

Toss the blackberries into the slow cooker after they've been rinsed. Sugar, cornstarch, and melted butter are sprinkled over the top. Combine the ingredients in a mixing bowl. Stir together the dry ingredients mentioned in the cobbler layer above in a medium-sized mixing basin. After that, combine the wet ingredients. Stir until thoroughly blended; some lumps are acceptable; do not overmix. Pour the batter evenly over the blackberries. Combine the sugar and cinnamon in a small mixing dish. This should be sprinkled over the batter. Cover the slow cooker with the lid. Cook for 2 hours and 30 minutes on high. During the cooking process, do not open the lid. Serve with a dollop of ice cream or whipped cream on top.

Nutrients: Kcal 274, Fat: 7g, Total Carbs: 49g, Protein: 4g

13. Peanut Butter Blondies

Prep time: 20 minutes

Cook time: 1 hour 30 minutes

Servings: 12

Ingredients

- 8.3 oz of all-purpose flour
- 1/4 tsp baking powder
- 2.1 oz of sugar
- 3 tbsp of brown sugar
- 2 tbsp of butter
- 2 tbsp of peanut butter
- 1 large egg
- 1 tsp of vanilla
- 19.2 oz of chocolate chips

Instructions

Grease the interior of your slow cooker well with butter. Then sprinkle a little flour on top and tilt the pan to coat the edges and bottom. Remove any extra flour with a dump shovel. Whisk together the flour and baking powder in a mixing dish and set it aside. Combine the butter, peanut butter, sugar, and brown sugar in an electric mixer on medium speed until light and creamy. Incorporate the egg until it is completely incorporated. Blend in the vanilla extract until the mixture is completely smooth. With the spatula, gradually fold in the flour mixture until it's just combined. Stir in the chocolate chunks gently. Scrape the batter into the slow cooker and smooth it up. Set the lid on the slow cooker and cover it with several layers of paper towels. Cook for 1 to 2 hours on high mode. Remove the insert from the cooker and cool it for about 30 minutes on a wire rack. Cut the cake into pieces and serve.

Nutrients: Kcal 148, Fat: 7.3g, Total Carbs: 19.8g, Protein: 2.6g

14. Nut Clusters

Prep time: 5 minutes

Cook time: 1 hour 30 minutes

Servings: 35

Ingredients

- 2 pounds of salted dry roasted peanuts
- 11.5 oz of milk chocolate chips
- 11.5 oz of semi-sweet chocolate chips
- 11.5 oz of white chocolate chips
- 10 oz of peanut butter chips

Instructions

In the slow cooker, combine the peanuts and baking chips. Cover a slow cooker with the lid. Cook for roughly 1 to 2 hours on low. Stir regularly. Because this is genuine chocolate, it will burn if left too long. After the chocolate has completely melted, turn off the slow cooker. Remove the insert from the base and place it on potholders. Preheat oven to 350°F. Line three baking pans with parchment or wax paper. Scoop the batter onto cookie sheets that have been prepared with parchment paper. Use one to scoop and the other to scrape the batter into the pans. Make a flat cookie form out of the ingredients. If desired, garnish with sprinkles.

Nutrients: Kcal 336, Fat: 23g, Total Carbs: 26g, Protein: 9g

15. Mixed Berry Cake

Prep time: 15 minutes

Cook time: 4 hours

Servings: 16

Ingredients

- 17 oz of blueberries
- 17 oz of raspberries
- 17 oz of blackberries
- 4.2 oz of sugar
- 3 oz of raspberry-flavored gelatin
- 1 box white cake mix
- 8.3 fl oz of water
- 2.8 oz of butter
- Whipped cream to garnish

Instructions

Rinse the berries and pat them dry. Fill the baking dish halfway with berries. Sugar and gelatin are sprinkled on top. Using a mixer, blend the butter, cake mix and water until smooth. Pour the cake batter over the fruit and spread it out evenly. Bake for 4 hours on high, or until cake is completely done. Warm whipped cream is served on top.

Nutrients: Kcal 200, Fat: 9g, Total Carbs: 29g, Protein: 2g

16. Fudge Bars

Prep time: 15 minutes

Cook time: 1 hour

Servings: 30

Ingredients

- 14.1 oz of chocolate chips
- 14.1 oz of sweetened condensed milk
- 1 tsp of vanilla essence
- 0.5 oz of unsalted butter

Instructions

Grease and line a baking pan with parchment paper. In a slow cooker, combine all of the ingredients. Reduce the heat to low and remove the lid from the slow cooker. Cook for one hour, stirring about 15-30 minutes in between. Pour into the lined tin when finished. Refrigerate for at least two hours. After it has hardened, cut it into squares and enjoy!

Nutrients: Kcal 136, Fat: 6.5g, Total Carbs: 17.2g, Protein: 2.3g

17. Spice Apple Sauce Cake

Prep time: 15 minutes

Cook time: 4 hours

Servings: 6

Ingredients

- 8.3 oz of flour
- 1/2 tsp of baking soda
- 1/4 tsp of cinnamon powder
- 1/2 tsp of nutmeg
- 1/2 tsp of cloves
- 4.1 oz of sugar
- 4.3 fl oz of unsweetened applesauce
- 1 egg
- 1/2 tsp of vanilla essence
- 6 tbsp of butter
- Sugar for confectioners

Instructions

Line a pan with parchment paper after greasing it. Place an aluminum foil rack in the bottom of the slow cooker and add water. Combine flour, cinnamon, cloves, nutmeg, and baking soda in a medium mixing basin. Whisk the sugar, applesauce, egg, vanilla, and salt in a large mixing basin until smooth and lump-free. Slowly whisk in the melted butter until it is thoroughly combined. In the slow cooker, place the cake pan on the aluminum rack, cover, and cook low for about 3 to 4 hours. Remove the pan from the crock and set it on a wire rack to cool entirely for about 1 to 2 hours. Remove the bottom of the cake pan and discard the parchment paper. Place the cake in a serving dish and dust with confectioners' sugar before slicing and serving.

Nutrients: Kcal 271, Fat: 12.5g, Total Carbs: 37g, Protein: 3.5g

18. Peachy Cobbler

Prep time: 30 minutes

Cook time: 2 hours

Servings: 10

Ingredients

- 8 medium peaches - 10.4 oz of sugar
- 6.2 oz of wheat flour
- 4.2 oz of all-purpose flour
- 2 tsp of baking powder
- 1/4 tsp of salt - 1/2 tsp of baking soda
- 4.3 fl oz unsalted butter - Vanilla ice cream

Instructions

To peel the peaches fast and simply, bring a big pot of water to a boil with enough water to cover the peaches. Once the water is boiling, gently lower the peaches into the water using a slotted spoon or tongs to protect your fingers. 1 minute at a boil to stop the cooking, remove the peaches from the pot and place them in an ice bath. Peaches should be cut into slices and placed in a large mixing dish. Spray a slow cooker lightly with cooking spray. Gently stir sugar in to coat the peaches. Place the peaches in the slow cooker, along with any liquids. Combine the remaining sugar, white whole wheat flour, all-purpose flour, baking powder, baking soda, and salt in a separate dish. Spread the sugar evenly over the peaches, then lay the butter slices on top. Cook for about 2-3 hours on high or about 4 hours on low, until the peaches are soft and gently browned on top. Serve warm with a scoop of vanilla ice cream, a dollop of Greek yogurt, or a dollop of heavy cream on top.

Nutrients: Kcal 264, Fat: 10g, Total Carbs: 44g, Protein: 3g

19. Coffee Cake

Prep time: 15 minutes

Cook time: 2 hours

Servings: 8

Ingredients

For Topping

- 4.2 oz of white sugar
- 2.1 oz of flour
- 2.1 oz cup of butter
- 1 tsp of cinnamon

For Cake Batter

- 12.5 oz of flour
- 2 tsp of baking powder
- 1/2 tsp of salt
- 1 egg
- 6.2 oz of sugar
- 2.8 fl oz of butter
- 4.2 fl oz of milk
- 1 tsp of vanilla

Instructions

Spray your slow cooker with nonstick cooking spray or grease it. Combine the sugar, flour, butter, and cinnamon in a small mixing basin to make the crumb topping. Set aside after softly mixing with a fork until crumbs. To make the batter, whisk together the flour, baking powder, and salt; put aside. Whisk the egg in a medium mixing basin until it is foamy. Then, when fully blended, add the sugar and melted butter. Pour in the milk and vanilla extract. Mix in the flour mixture with a wooden spoon until everything is completely blended. Pour into a slow cooker that has been oiled. Cover the slow cooker with a double layer of paper towels. Cook on high for about 2 hours, then check with a toothpick to see whether it's done. Cut and serve.

Nutrients: Kcal 263, Fat: 15g, Total Carbs: 29g, Protein: 4.3g

20. Caramel Cream Dessert

Prep time: 25 minutes

Cook time: 3 hours

Servings: 6

Ingredients

- 20.3 fl oz of fat milk
- 1 vanilla pod
- 160g golden caster sugar
- 1.9 fl oz of water
- 4 egg yolks
- 2 eggs

Instructions

Set the slow cooker to low heat. Grease ramekin dishes with cooking spray. Combine the milk and vanilla pod in a saucepan over medium heat and bring to a boil. Remove from the fire and set aside for about 45 minutes to cool. Meanwhile, in a second small saucepan, combine half of the sugar with water and slowly bring to a boil. Cook for around 10 to 15 minutes, or until the sugar has completely dissolved and caramelized. Divide the caramelized sugar evenly among the ramekins that have been prepared. Combine the remaining sugar, egg yolks, and whole eggs in a mixing dish and whisk until light and creamy. Add the cooled vanilla milk to the mixture in a slow, steady stream, whisking constantly. Using kitchen twine, secure the ramekins with tin foil. Fill the ramekins halfway with boiling water and place them in the prepared slow cooker. Cook for about 3 hours with the lid on. Remove the ramekins from the water and set them aside to cool for around 2 to 3 hours at room temperature. Place in the fridge overnight once it has cooled. Invert over a serving plate and tap out to serve.

Nutrients: Kcal 222, Fat: 6.2g, Total Carbs: 35g, Protein: 6.9g

21. Apple Puree

Prep time: 20 minutes

Cook time: 2 hours

Servings: 18

Ingredients

- 30 oz of fresh stevia leaves
- 20.3 fl oz of boiling water
- 35.3 oz of cooking apples

Instructions

Combine the boiling water and the fresh stevia leaves in a mixing basin. Remove the stevia leaves and discard them. Preheat the slow cooker to the lowest setting. Combine the stevia-infused water and apples in a saucepan over medium heat. Bring to a mild simmer, then transfer to a slow cooker and cook for about 3 to 4 hours on low. Remove the slow cooker from the heat and mix with a hand-held liquidizer. Serve immediately or freeze for later use.

Nutrients: Kcal 54, Fat: 0.1g, Total Carbs: 13g, Protein: 0.1g

22. Peanut Butter and Chocolate Pudding

Prep time: 15 minutes

Cook time: 1 hour 45 minutes

Servings: 12

Ingredients

- 7.1 oz of flour
- 2.6 oz of brown sugar
- 1 tsp of soda
- 1 tsp baking powder
- 8.8 oz of peanut butter
- 6.2 oz of soured cream
- 1 tsp almond extract
- 3 tbsp of butter
- 2 tbsp of boiling water
- 5.3 oz of caster sugar
- 1 oz of cocoa powder
- 16.9 fl oz of boiling water
- 1 tbsp chocolate syrup

Instructions

Using cooking spray, coat the inside of a slow cooker. In a mixing dish, combine flour, brown sugar, baking powder, and bicarbonate of soda. In a separate bowl, whisk together peanut butter, soured cream, melted butter, almond essence, and hot water until smooth. To get a very thick consistency, stir the flour mixture into the peanut butter mixture. Place the ingredients in the slow cooker that has been prepared. In a mixing basin, whisk together white sugar, cocoa powder, and boiling water until smooth. In a slow cooker, pour the chocolate mixture over the pudding. Cook on high for around 1 to 2 hours, or until the pudding begins to peel away from the sides of the cooker and feels firm on top. Allow around 15 minutes for cooling before serving. Drizzle with chocolate syrup.

Nutrients: Kcal 200, Fat: 8g, Total Carbs: 27g, Protein: 5g

23. Coconut Cake

Prep time: 30 minutes

Cook time: 3 hours

Servings: 8

Ingredients

For Cake

- 7.1 oz of caster sugar
- 4.1 fl oz of coconut oil
- 4.2 oz of unsalted butter
- 3 eggs
- 8.8 oz of plain flour
- 1 tsp of baking powder
- 1/4 tsp of salt
- 4.1 fl oz of coconut milk

For Icing

- 4.2 oz of cream cheese
- 2.1 oz of unsalted butter
- 6.3 oz of icing sugar
- 1/4 of salt
- 1/2 tsp of vanilla extract
- 4.2 oz of coconut flakes

Instructions

In a large mixing basin, blend the sugar, coconut oil, and butter with an electric mixer until completely incorporated. 1 at a time, add eggs, beating well after each addition. In a mixing basin, combine flour, baking powder, and salt. Whisk the flour mixture and coconut milk into the butter mixture until barely incorporated. Line the bottom of your slow cooker with parchment paper and generously grease the ceramic bowl with butter or cooking spray. Evenly spread cake batter on top of the parchment paper. Cook on high for about 1 to 2 hours. Remove the lid as well as the kitchen towel. Remove the ceramic dish and set it aside to cool for about 10 minutes. To make the icing, whisk cream cheese and butter in a mixing basin with an electric mixer on high speed for about 3 minutes, or until light and fluffy. Mix in the salt and vanilla extract. Top the cake with a layer of icing and toasted coconut flakes.

Nutrients: Kcal 399, Fat: 12g, Total Carbs: 71g, Protein: 4.9g

24. Cream Brulee

Prep time: 10 minutes

Cook time: 2 hours 5 minutes

Servings: 4

Ingredients

- 4 egg yolks
- 1.8 oz of caster sugar
- 1/4 tsp of salt
- 2 tsp of vanilla extract
- 13.5 fl oz of double cream
- 4 tsp of caster sugar

Instructions

Whisk together the yolks, sugar, salt, and vanilla extract in a mixing bowl, then slowly whisk in the cream. Using a strainer, strain the mixture into a measuring jug. To prevent ramekins from sliding around, line the bottom of a slow oval cooker with a folded piece of kitchen roll. On top of the kitchen roll, place ramekins. Fill the slow cooker halfway up the sides of the ramekins with water. Fill ramekins halfway with custard. Cover the top of the slow cooker with a kitchen roll, then cover with the lid. Cook on low for about 2 hours, or until the custard is set but still jiggles slightly. Allow about 45 minutes for ramekins to cool completely on a rack. Chill the custards for at least 3 hours, uncovered. Serve immediately after browning the sugar.

Nutrients: Kcal 320, Fat: 1.6g, Total Carbs: 17.5g, Protein: 4.4g

25. Peach Cake

Prep time: 30 minutes

Cook time: 2 hours 50 minutes

Servings: 8

Ingredients

- 3 tin peaches
- 2.4 oz of butter
- 5.1 oz of brown sugar
- 12.3 oz of butter
- 7.1 oz of caster sugar
- 2 large eggs
- 8.8 oz of flour
- 2 tsp of baking powder
- 1/2 tsp of salt
- 1 tsp of cinnamon
- 1/2 tsp of nutmeg
- 1/2 tsp of almond extract
- 8.1 fl oz of milk

Instructions

Allow for about 20 minutes for peach slices to dry between several layers of kitchen roll. In the meantime, melt the butter and pour it into the bottom of the slow cooker's ceramic bowl. In a bowl, combine brown sugar, cinnamon, and nutmeg, then sprinkle over the butter. Over brown sugar, arrange peaches in a compact layer. In a large mixing bowl, beat softened butter and caster sugar with an electric mixer until light and fluffy, about 3 minutes. Beat in the eggs well after each addition. Add the almond extract and mix well. In a separate basin, combine flour, baking powder, and salt. Working in batches, alternating the flour mixture and milk into egg mixture, beginning and finishing with flour mixture. Combine all of the ingredients in a mixing bowl and stir until everything is completely blended. Using a spoon, evenly distribute the sauce over the peaches. Cover the top of the slow cooker with a kitchen roll to collect any moisture while baking, then cover with the lid. Cook on High for about 2 hours or until a skewer inserted into the center of the cake comes out clean. Set it aside to cool for around 10 minutes. Cut around the edge of the cake with a knife and carefully flip out onto a serving dish.

Nutrients: Kcal 227, Fat: 11g, Total Carbs: 31g, Protein: 3.1g

Conclusion

Slow cookers have several advantages, including that they are simple to use and allow for hands-off cooking. With a slow cooker, all you have to do is combine all of your ingredients and leave your meal to cook while you're away from the kitchen. It can be extremely useful in having delicious meals ready for you and your family. The ability to prepare a meal in the slow cooker minimizes the temptation to takeout, which is frequently less nutritious and more expensive. Slow cookers, for the most part, allow for one-step preparation. Preparation time is reduced, and cleanup time is reduced by combining all of the ingredients in a slow cooker. Slow cookers come in handy at all times of the year. When you come in from a chilly winter day, the smell of heated soup is a welcome sight. These cookers are ideal for summertime use because they do not generate as much heat in the kitchen as an oven. They aid in the tenderization of less expensive pieces of meat due to the long, low-temperature cooking time. With a slow cooker, you can bring out the flavors in your cuisine. You can cook various items using this cooker, including one-pot dinners, soups, stews, and gratins, among others. When compared to an oven, a slow cooker consumes less electricity. If you are concerned about leaving it on and cooking while away from home for most of the day, consider cooking dishes at alternate hours when you are home, including while sleeping. When the items are finished cooking, allow them to cool before keeping them in the refrigerator until they are ready to be reheated in the stovetop or oven for a later meal. Slow cookers are beneficial because they cook food at a low temperature, which reduces the likelihood of nutrient destruction compared to other cooking methods. Crockpots are also beneficial to one's health because most slow cooker recipes make extensive use of natural ingredients and broths. In contrast to grilling, roasting, and other high-temperature cooking methods that rely on flavorings and additives, slow cooker cooking relies almost entirely on organic ingredients. Ingredients such as veggies, potatoes, and powdered spices enhance the flavor of these meals, among other things. As a result, eating foods prepared in them regularly will improve your overall health and help reduce your intake of potentially dangerous ingredients.

Printed in Great Britain
by Amazon